Meeting and Event Planning Playbook

Meeting Planning Fundamentals

A Quick Reference Guide
for
Administrative Assistants,
Coordinators, and
New Meeting Planners
who need to plan corporate meetings

D1301388

Scholar
Consulting
Group, LLC

Trusted Advisors and Superior Solutions
for the Travel and Meetings Market

By Debi Scholar and Susan Losurdo

Barrel Maker Publishing
2013

ISBN-13: 978-1489572905
ISBN-10: 1489572902
ISBN: 978-0-9834397-8-3 (ebk)
ISBN: 978-0-9834397-9-0 (pbk)

Book cover designed by: one3graphix http://www.one3graphix.com
Book interiors designed by: Reality Infosystems http://www.realityinfo.com

Table of Contents

Endorsements

Debi is an engaging and highly skilled meetings and events professional. Her advice and recommendations are based on years of relevant experience and highly valued by her clients and peers. Listen to her – she can help you take your program to top performance!

Bev Heinritz
Vice President
Client Development
Dinova
Corporate Dining Connection

Debi Scholar is a creative, solutions-oriented professional who delivers significant value to her clients. By first considering how best to support clients' business goals, she develops and executes meetings and events that help participants focus their attention on outcomes rather than mere process, while still creating an atmosphere that facilitates fun and creativity. Her passion for her field is infectious, and she is a dynamic speaker on the subject of how strategic event planning and management lead to business success.

Bobby Badalamenti
Director
Siemens Event Management Services
Siemens Corporation

Debi has been dedicated for years to elevating the profession of meeting and event planning. This resource is an excellent reference for those tasked to plan a meeting in adjunct to their regular duties. It is also a great quick reference for those who have planned meetings for years. Debi's ability to quickly and clearly get to the heart of what needs to be accomplished is a great gift that she shares with this reference guide.

Kudos to Debi for another job well done.

Madlyn Caliri
Director, Global Procurement
Hotels, Meetings and Exhibitions
Reed Elsevier

One of the things I like most about Debi's approach is that speaks to the masses regardless of how long you've been planning meetings; In fact, as a 30+ veteran, there were areas that assisted me with designing a recent meeting in New York. I also commend Debi on the logical way it's been presented and the fact that it covers all of the various challenges that we face when planning a meeting. Great job Debi!

Ken Edwards
National Account Executive
SmartSource Rentals

As an executive coach who works with many clients in the meetings and events industry, I strongly advocate the position that there are two fundamental factors that determine the level to which an employee will manifest their own personal peak performance: attitude and aptitude. While attitude is often a complex result of personal and professional experiences, one of the simplest (and most powerful) ways of driving appropriate levels of aptitude is to provide employees with the best tools available in the market to do their jobs. In my opinion, the Meeting Planning Playbook is one of the most relevant tools I've seen in a long time for anyone with responsibility for the planning of an event on behalf of their organization for three reasons: 1) It is intelligently and logically laid out, 2) the content is exceptionally thorough yet concisely presented, and 3) the robust sources of additional information increases the value of the playbook exponentially. I highly recommend this book as a 'must-have' resource tool to keep close at hand and reference often. Think of it as an 'aptitude enhancer' for anyone tasked with planning an event for their organization.

Mike Malinchok
President
S2K Performance Coaching, LLC

Debi's writings have always been must-read in our industry. Her current book is a resource not only for corporate and independent meeting planners, but is also equally valuable to Executive Assistants, Communications Directors and anyone tasked with delivering meeting ROI. Afterburner will consider it required reading for all new hires, and is including it as a resource for our entire team – rookies and veterans alike!

Scott Leonard
VP, Business Development
Afterburner, Inc.

As a supplier in the meeting planning industry who helps support many clients manage the myriad of meeting details, this is a "must read" playbook for anyone tasked with the responsibility for planning a meeting for their organization. Debi has the uncanny ability to take her skills, talent and expertise and translate it into a well-scripted document that is clear, concise and manageable. I applaud Debi for bringing this information to us. She continues to make the meeting industry a brighter and better place for all of us. Congratulations Debi, on another successful playbook.

Jody Wallace
President, CEO & Founder
EMCVenues
Your Complete Source Events, Meetings, Conferences

I hope every meeting and event planner or administrative assistant tasked with planning a meeting or event reads Debi's book. As a management consultant in the meetings and events industry, she truly is a Scholar in this field – no pun intended.

Scott Flynn
Founder and CEO
Best TeamBuilding and Corporate Events

I have been in the event business for 30 years, first as CEO of a large production and meeting planning company, and now as CEO of a leadership program business. I have often wondered 1) Why people with no training or experience (Admins, EAs, HR, etc) are given responsibility for planning and running an important meeting with no resources and 2) Why there are so few good aids to help these people. Debi has hit a sweet spot with this book – an array of guidelines, advice, checklists, and resources to make any meeting or event better. With the tools in this book at your disposal, any meeting or event can be made much much better.

Doug Keeley
CEO & Chief Storyteller
The Mark of a Leader

Acknowledgements

To Mom – Thank you for making me help you plan your Union Parties when I was a teenager. Miss you tremendously, love you forever. "Always stand up for what you believe in!"

To Laurynn and Justin – Thank you for being perfect kids, now perfect adults. Your birthday parties, Bat and Bar Mitzvahs were the most fun events to plan, as I watched you become young adults.

To David – As I was the Westinghouse training coordinator who planned the product school and cocktail party 26 years ago where we first met, thank you for supporting me all these years.

To Pat and Bill – Thank you for being my surrogate parents and helping me with everything now that mom is gone. You helped me get through the toughest year of my life.

To my Westinghouse Furniture Systems managers – Thank you for tasking me with all of the 1980s product and design schools that I planned for years, and for being sympathetic when I didn't understand why I received a hotel penalty from the Harley Hotel in Grand Rapids, Michigan for something called "attrition," a word that had no meaning to me in the 80s.

To Ayisha – You were the best colleague to work with at both Dean Witter and PricewaterhouseCoopers. You helped me with so many training meetings at both firms, I can't even begin to count. You're the best.

To my PricewaterhouseCoopers team – You are still the best team of meeting managers and planners ever, even though it looks different today. Thank you for working with me and teaching me. We excelled to great levels, all because of you. Susan, thank YOU for co-authoring this book.

To my colleagues and clients – Thank you for answering all of my questions over the years and allowing me to work with you.

I wrote my first rhyme when I was 6 or 7 years old. Since then, I have written hundreds of short rhymes; enjoy this one as it relates to planning meetings.

Planning Meetings

Details overflow on our tablet at hand
Obscure requirements they want us to plan
Nausea sets in as we only have weeks
Attendees expect a meeting that's unique

Leap into action and get a hotel
Décor and entertainment, "We expect you to excel!"
Contracts and clauses through legal review
Marked revisions and too much to do
Air transportation, food, and ground
Tasks, emails, and numbers abound

Humor and patience are keys to success
Even though we all need time to de-stress
We can help you, so take a look
Sharpen your knowledge and use this Playbook

By Debi Scholar

To my crazy and perfect son Enzo:

My apologies in advance as I will plan each and every one of your birthday parties, school fundraisers, graduations, and any other celebrations in your life as if it was a marquee event. There will be project plans, budgets, marketing communications, menu development, checklists, show flows, volunteers, etc. It will drive you crazy, just ask your father. Just know that I do it with love. Your mother is now, and forever will be, a Professional Event Manager.

I love you with all of my heart.

"Put it in the basket, Put it in the basket, Put it in the basket won't you please."

By Susan Losurdo

About the Authors

Debi Scholar, President of Scholar Consulting Group (SCG), is a consultant, strategist, speaker, educator, and author. Her "10,000 foot level" vision and her operational "roll up your sleeves approach" steers her passion for delivering exceptional quality service to her Clients who experience up to 25% savings, up to 75% risk reduction, and for those Clients that are suppliers, up to 300% increase in sales. Debi supports hundreds of corporate and association clients with their meetings and events, travel, card, expense, and training programs.

She authored Strategic Meetings Management (SMM): The Quick Reference Guide and co-authored The SMM Handbook. With eight designations, she is driven to constantly improve her expertise so that she can implement best practices with her clients. Debi created the industry's first SMM Maturity Model©, her must-read blog, T&E Plus, has been viewed over 40,000 times, and her T&E Plus LinkedIn Group has over 2,000 members. She also created the GBTA SMM LinkedIn Group that has over 1,000 members.

Before starting her own consultancy, Debi managed the PricewaterhouseCooper's (PwC) SMM Program and she was the first Meeting Director to have included Virtual Meetings under her direction back in 2002. She is a meeting strategist bridging the meeting content, architecture, and theming into successful, measurable meetings and events. Because she owned her own training company, was a Training Director at PwC, and a Training Manager at Dean Witter, Debi integrates all of her content development training skills along with logistics planning skills which brings multiple benefits to her Clients.

In 2013, Debi was named one of The 25 Most Influential People in the Meetings Industry by Successful Meetings Magazine. Debi was the co-chair of the GBTA Groups & Meetings Committee, a GBTA Foundation Board Member, an MCAF member, named a "Mover and Shaker" of the industry by *Corporate & Incentive Travel Magazine,* and was named a Top 20 Changemaker by *Corporate Meetings & Incentives Magazine* when she was the PricewaterhouseCoopers Director of Meetings, Events, and Group Travel.

Debi has the following designations Global Business Travel Association (GBTA) Global Leadership Professional (GLP), Global Travel Professional (GTP), Corporate Travel Expert (CTE), Certificate in Meetings Management (CMM), Certified Meeting Professional (CMP), Six Sigma Green Belt (SSGB), Certified Technical Trainer (CTT), and Certified BANK™ Sales Trainer (CBST).

Debi can be reached at 1-908-304-4954 or at Debi@DebiScholar.com.

Susan N Losurdo, CMP, LES is a Global Meeting & Event Management Professional with over 15 years of extensive experience as both a Corporate Meeting Manager, Planner and a Hotel Supplier.

Currently, Susan has taken on the role of Vice President at The Scholar Consulting Group (SCG). Her main function is to oversee the Meeting & Event Operations arm of the Group by managing seamless events for SCG clients. At a higher level - Susan understands and promotes the Strategic Meetings Management Program (SMMP) philosophy. She uses this knowledge to analyze and compile client meeting data in order to provide organizations a better understanding of how SMMP can benefit them. Susan has co-authored the "Meeting & Event Planning Playbook" as well as a "Crisis Management Guide". She speaks and instructs at the university level on topics related to hospitality and event management.

Prior to her work at The Scholar Consulting Group, Susan had the opportunity to learn and excel in various other meeting management roles. She has worked as a corporate meeting planner (Global Meeting & Event Manager - PricewaterhouseCoopers, LLP) and as a third party meeting planner (Experient - Onsite at Cisco Technologies - Manager, Meeting & Event Operations - Team Lead North America). Susan even worked as a meeting supplier (Hyatt Hotels - Sales, Catering, and Convention Services). This breadth of experience positions her well to understand various perspectives and partner well with her clients.

Planning meetings and events from end-to-end, managing teams, mentoring and training staff, reporting, consulting, teaching, writing ... all are things Susan is passionate about.

Susan is a member of Meeting Professionals International (MPI) as well as International Association of Protocol Consultants (IAPC). She holds a Bachelor of Business Administration degree in Marketing from the University of Wisconsin - Madison.

Susan holds the following professional designations: Certified Meeting Professional (CMP) and Learning Environmental Specialist (LES)

Susan can be reached at salosurdo@gmail.com.

About the Playbook

IMPORTANT: IT IS EXTREMELY IMPORTANT to use professional meeting planners for meetings valued over $10,000. (Some organizations use $5,000 as the threshold for using professional meeting planners). Check with your organization to find out if you have professional meeting planners that can assist you. Professional meeting planners know how to align the business objectives with the content of the meeting as well as reduce the costs and risks. It is best if you use a professional meeting planner to negotiate contracts. Look for a Certified Meeting Professional (CMP). If you are not sure where to find a professional meeting planner, contact Debi, Susan, or Meeting Professionals International at www.mpiweb.org.

There are many meeting planning books and websites available that use far more comprehensive forms and methods than what you will find in this Playbook. For example, on the Accepted Practices EXchange (APEX) website, (http://www.conventionindustry. org/StandardsPractices/APEX.aspx) you will find numerous templates. This Playbook is not designed to replace any of those wonderful resources. Instead, this Playbook is meant to be an easy-to-read quick reference guide for those people who need to plan small meetings. We offer some quick options and forms, but the documents at APEX are standards in the industry.

This guide has been prepared as a tool to assist you in planning and executing productive and effective meetings and events. Open-ended questioning, careful planning, good organization, strict scheduling, interesting topics and speakers, and lead-time are all integral elements of a successful meeting or event.

Professional meeting planners use checklists that are sometimes 40-50 pages in length if not more. This Meeting and Event Planning Playbook is not meant to replace the professional meeting planners' checklists but rather is designed to support those ad hoc meeting planners who occasionally plan meetings or events.

Administrative assistants, coordinators, managers and many other people are often asked, "Will you please help me plan my meeting or event?" The people who ask you to plan their meeting or event do not usually realize how long it may take you to perform these activities. Sometimes, they do not give you enough time, do not tell you how much money you have to spend, or give you all of the details.

Did you ever notice how important details that support the meeting are not shared until the middle of your planning? This Meeting and Event Planning Playbook will provide you with a quick reference guide checklist and the questions to ask in order to plan a successful meeting or event.

Who should use the Playbook

This Meeting and Event Planning Playbook is designed for:

- Administrative Assistants, Coordinators, and Managers who plan meetings
- Meeting Managers and Planners who want to provide an Administrative Assistant with a reference guide if they are self-planning meetings
- Travel managers who want to learn more about the category of meeting and event planning
- Anyone else who is new to meetings and events

Defining Meetings and Events

What is the difference between a meeting and an event?

Meetings are defined differently by organizations yet sometimes meetings are not defined at all. Some people differentiate between meetings and events while others use the terms interchangeably. Meetings may be one or several days in length. Meetings often include numerous events that must be integrated to provide a seamless experience for the attendees. No two meetings or events are alike.

Whereas a meeting may be a workshop, project team meeting, training session, retreat, or conference, an event may be a client reception, town hall meeting, entertainment event, a team-building activity, a fundraiser, or dinner event. Events are often a few hours to one day in length. Yet, multi-day events may often be the most challenging and offer the greatest return on investment, as with the case of planning for a golf invitational event that includes high-profile clients.

Yet, there may be people who disagree with this definition of a "meeting" vs. an "event."

Organizations that manage their meetings strategically (called Strategic Meetings Management "SMM"[1]) may define a "meeting" as one or more of the following:

- Any meeting or event that requires any type of contract
- Any meeting or event that requires ten or more sleeping rooms
- Any meeting or event that costs more than $X (sometimes $5,000, $10,000 or $25,000).

Some organizations may use different definitions and some have not defined meetings at all. Some organizations require that meetings that fall into the above categories be planned by professional meeting planners, often staff that have earned the designation of a Certified Meeting Professional (CMP) and / or a Certificate in Meetings Management (CMM). Sometimes meetings with less than 10 attendees may be procured and planned by an administrative assistant or a coordinator.

Whether your meeting or event is held on your organization's property, or off-site at a hotel or a different type of venue, meeting and event planning requires preparation, attention to detail, and dedication to ensure a successful attendee experience.

Throughout this Playbook, the word "meeting" refers to a meeting or an event.

---

1   Strategic Meetings Management provides direction to guide the strategy, operations and tactical activities of meetings and events in order to improve business processes, quality, and return on investment, and reduce costs, risks and inefficiencies, as per the "Strategic Meetings Management: The Strategy Quick Reference Guide."

Logistics vs. Content

A meeting or event requires a project manager or someone who can oversee and plan the:

a) meeting / event logistics

b) meeting / event content

First, let's define the logistics: Logistics, in meeting and event planning, is defined as managing and planning the end-to-end details of the meeting, with the tasks to obtain a location, plan for travel, determine the quantity of sleeping rooms needed, plan the food and beverage service, secure the audiovisual needs, and ground transportation to and from the airport.

Second, let's define the content: Content, in meeting and event planning, is defined as the reason why the meeting or event is occurring, as well as the information delivered throughout the agenda. For example, content may be to host a team-building activity, brainstorm ideas for a new project, deliver a presentation to salespeople, or create a memorable experience as an incentive trip awarded for superior performance.

This Meeting and Event Planning Playbook is designed for readers who need to plan logistics and has very little information on content creation. However, when you plan a meeting or event, it is important to know what the content will include so that you can identify the right venue, reserve the right type of room(s), and plan for the right type of off-site activities.

For more information on content, sometimes called the meeting architecture, please refer to Appendix.

Before the Planning Begins

1. **Know your experts**

   Before you get started, find out if your organization has professional meeting planners on staff, or professional meeting planning suppliers that can help you. These invaluable resources can save you money, time and frustration. Some organizations may have a Meeting Policy that communicates when to use these professional resources and how they will support your meeting. If your organization does not have professional resources to help you, then you may want to find the right professional organization to help you through the resources at Meeting Professionals International.[2]

2. **Why it is important to use professional meeting planners**

   Professional meeting planners are educated on where to hold meetings, how to reduce costs and risks through negotiations and preferred contractual terms, when to use unique venues such as museums, why meetings should provide a return on investment, how to use efficient tools, processes and templates to expedite the planning stages, and how to plan for crises that occur. Professional meeting planners will work side by side with you to help you achieve your meeting goals and make you look like a star.

3. **Find out if your organization has a meeting policy**

   Many organizations have developed a meeting policy that states who can plan meetings, what suppliers must be used, who can sign contracts, how to plan a meeting / event, what ethical practices must be followed, and when a request for proposal must be used. Find out if your organization has a meeting policy, and always abide by those guidelines.

4. **Ask the right questions**

   It is helpful to get the following questions answered up front. It is a good practice to gain as much information as possible to reduce the chance of reworking your planning activities. This Playbook provides you with a list of questions to ask your meeting requester throughout the guide as well as in the Appendix.

---

2   Meeting Professionals International at www.MPIWEB.org.

Professional Meeting Planning Services

Professional meeting planners can assist you with:

1. Project management

2. Site consultation, selection, negotiation and contracting

3. Virtual and hybrid meetings

4. Invitation / Registration / RSVP Management

5. Attendee management / rooming list assistance through the use of automated technologies

6. Communications to attendees, suppliers, leaders, IT, support staff

7. Logistics planning (meeting rooms, food and beverage, audio-visual, technology requirements, off-site activities, etc.)

8. Air / ground transportation

9. Content development / facilitation / speakers

10. On-site management and assistance

11. Event Marketing / Branding

12. Social Media

13. Invoice review and reconciliation

14. Metrics and Reporting

Notes

Professional Meeting Planner Contacts

Name, Email, Phone:

Name, Email, Phone:

Name, Email, Phone:

Other Notes:

Types of Risks with Meetings

The planning of meetings and events requires complex activities, numerous suppliers, multiple resources, and risk mitigation, and results in significant spend. An average meeting produces three contracts (e.g., hotel, ground transportation, audio-visual, activities, etc.). Many meetings / events are extremely visible to leaders and require high-touch services by numerous planners. In contrast, some meetings fall below the detectable visibility of management and are considered small meetings / events. Yet even the small meetings / events pose risks, use valuable resources and when aggregated, result in high expenses for organizations. Meetings pose significant risks that professional meeting planners usually know how to mitigate. These risks include:

Risk Exposure Category	Types of Risk
Reputation The risk of not meeting the strategic objectives of the organization which may arise from negative public opinion.	- Meetings/events held without purpose and in conflict with organization's principles which may result in negative public perception - Employees asking for or accepting free services in the hospitality industry
Business Operations The risk that the organization structure, manual and automated processes, procedures and controls are not designed or functioning as designed to support the organization's SMM objectives	- Failure to help staff, or know where staff are, in times of crisis - Physical risk / personal safety - Multiple leaders on one aircraft - Ad hoc planner pays invoices for a fictitious meeting planning company and pockets the money
Regulatory/Legal Risk The risk of not meeting the strategic objectives of the organization arising from the company's failure to comply with external laws and regulations	- Company pays fine for loss of private information - Auditor cannot locate contracts or invoices for services and deems the activity unauditable - Important documents (e.g. contracts) may not be held for a required period (often 5 or 7 years) - Insurance rider for team building event was not garnered and someone gets hurt
Information Technology The risk of not meeting the strategic objectives of the organization arising from the inability to implement efficient and effective information systems.	- Disparate data such as meeting attendees, contracts, and costs in an email system, disparate database or file cabinet rather than in the meeting management technology - Personal Identifiable Information (PII) may be sent through email without encryption; fees or fines could be incurred if data ends up in the wrong hands - Available penalty credits may not be displayed throughout organization and money is lost

Risk Exposure Category	Types of Risk
Market Risk The risk of not meeting the strategic objectives of the organization arising from the inability to adapt to changing external factors and service the customers.	- Customers do not receive quality treatment for meetings/events - Organization fails to recognize that the economic environment may require more prudent spending - Organization fails to properly brand meeting/event
Financial Risk The risk of not meeting the financial objectives of the organization arising from the inability to manage financial obligations and risks	- Loss of savings from lack of aggressive negotiations or loss of credits - Loss of cost avoidance from lack of concessions in contracts - Loss of reclaiming VAT - Failure to recognize invoice errors - Failure to manage demand of services and meeting volume

As you are planning your meeting, if you are unsure how to mitigate the above risks, please contact a professional meeting planner immediately, a legal / risk professional in your organization, or the authors.

Check the Calendar

Finding the right dates for your meeting may be challenging based on holidays – national or interfaith. Check holiday schedules to be sure that your meeting does not conflict with holidays. Three resources that may help you are:

National Holiday Schedule: http://www.timeanddate.com/holidays/us/

Interfaith Holiday Schedule: http://www.interfaithcalendar.org/

Global Holiday Schedule: http://www.timeanddate.com/holidays/

Other Meetings may also conflict with your meeting schedule. When organizations use meeting management tools to capture all of their meetings, it is possible to look at the calendar to ensure that your meeting does not overlap. Without a meeting management calendar, it is wise to check with key business units and departments to ensure that your meeting is held during a time without other meeting conflicts.

Your competitors are most likely hosting similar events. Efforts should be made to make sure your events and your competitors events do not conflict. This is especially important when you are hosting large client events as your attendance may suffer if your event takes place at the same time as your competitors.

Also consider the events that may be occurring in your chosen city over your meeting dates. For example, are there large conventions in town that may be consuming a great deal of hotel rooms and meeting space? Perhaps there is an annual city festival that draws large crowds and tourists. Events like this can deplete hotel room inventory, restaurant offerings, vendor availability, ease of public transport, etc.

Meeting Objectives

If you understand the purpose of the meeting and the expected outcome, then you can plan the meeting with an understanding of the expectations and plan for success.

Meetings or events are generally held to communicate, motivate, educate, celebrate, generate revenue or regenerate the workforce. The following table describes some meeting types, the purpose or goals of the meeting, a question to ask to develop ideas on measurement, and sample measurement ideas. Many organizations require that the meeting sponsor or budget holder be responsible for ensuring that the meeting expenses are valid, reasonable and necessary to achieve the desired business objectives.

You may also want to offer virtual meeting options to replace or complement meetings when the objective is to communicate, educate or generate revenue. Whereas, it is more challenging to use virtual technologies to motivate and celebrate.

- What is the meeting objective?
- What is the general purpose of the meeting?
- What do you hope to accomplish?
- What is the expected outcome and how will it be measured?
- Do you require a baseline of information before the meeting / event starts so that you can compare the information to the after-meeting results?

Return on Objective Measurement

Meeting Type Examples	Goal or Purpose of the Meeting	Question to ask to understand how to measure the outcome of the meeting or event	Measurement
Business, committee meeting	Communicate	Was the communication used and understood?	Measure the effects of the communication efforts. For example, if a business meeting was held to discuss a new project, the measurement could be the success of the project completion as evaluated by the project sponsor.
Product launch	Motivate	Did the attendees change or improve behavior through motivation?	Measure the effects of the improved behavior such as the familiarity of the new product or service before and after the meeting. Later, more measurements could be tracked such as increased sales of the product or service.

Meeting Type Examples	Goal or Purpose of the Meeting	Question to ask to understand how to measure the outcome of the meeting or event	Measurement
Training session	Educate	Did the attendees learn something that would reduce cost or risk, improve productivity or quality, or generate more sales?	Measure the effects of the education, including an increase in productivity after learning the new skill, or an increase in sales after learning about the product or service. If you are educating managers on how to "improve their management style" then you could measure the satisfaction of their staff, employee retention, attrition, etc.
Retreat, incentive type meeting	Celebrate	Did the attendees feel appreciated?	Measure the effects of the perceived value of the celebratory event. The measurement could be the increase in accomplishments throughout the year or the perceived feeling that the attendees had during the event.
Focus groups, Feedback meetings, Advisory councils	Evaluate	Did the attendees evaluate the service or product as expected and provide the needed feedback?	Measure the depth of the attendee feedback or the level of participation in advisory councils.
Sales meetings	Generate revenue	Did the event help generate more revenue?	Measure the effects of the leads generated, resulting sales or revenue generated.
Recruiting activities	Regenerate the workforce through recruiting	Did the organization hire more staff?	Measure the effects of the recruiting and interviewing efforts: the number of subsequent interviews held or the number hired who attended the job fair.

Meeting Effectiveness and Engagement

Have you ever wondered why some meetings or conferences are spectacular and some are so darn boring? Have you ever experienced Death by PowerPoint? What about that monotone presenter who never quits? Have you ever missed an industry convention because you were ill or the company did not have money for you to attend? Have you ever attended a conference and wandered from education session to education session hoping each one would be better than the last one?

All of these occurrences are the result of successful or unsuccessful meeting / event effectiveness and engagement. Ask yourself, did the content at your meeting work? Did the attendees get what they came for?

Meeting / event effectiveness and engagement quantifies the extent to which a desired outcome is achieved to meet or exceed the goals and objectives of the meeting. The Meeting Effectiveness and Engagement Quotient© measures the attendees experience in the pre-, during-, and post-meeting / event in 12 critical components. The higher the score, the higher the sense of accomplishment, satisfaction, ownership, and recurring participation by attendees. This comprehensive measurement of meeting effectiveness and engagement provides a roadmap for continuous improvement and a statistical model using scenario-based queries to articulate the value of moving forward with meeting effectiveness techniques.

Do you want attendees to score your event as "stellar," "perfect," and "can't wait to attend again!" Or, do you want them to think, "what a waste of time that meeting was!"

With a higher score in meeting effectiveness, an organization is more likely to achieve:

- greater sense of loyalty by attendees, speakers, and sponsors
- revitalization of meetings, events, and conferences
- improved attendance and assurance that the content meets the learning styles and generational style differences
- higher level of satisfaction
- improved revenue and sponsorships
- highly valued education
- improved business results (e.g. ROI, ROO, ROE)
- better quality of presenters / instructors who want to participate in your conferences
- strengthened relationships by attendees, speakers, and sponsors
- improved referrals for more membership opportunities
- supplementary and voluntary support for your organization

Debi uses a proprietary method to provide an organization with the roadmap and a detailed Meeting Effectiveness and Engagement Scorecard in the following 12 critical components.

To evaluate past meetings, Debi uses interviews, group sessions, review of materials, and surveys to measure meeting effectiveness in the pre-, during-, and post-meeting in 12 critical categories.

To improve upcoming meetings, Debi uses her instructional design and meeting strategy skills to develop the perfect meeting / event content ensuring that requirements in the 12 meeting effectiveness categories are met (or as many categories as the client wants to address).

The 12 Meeting Effectiveness and Engagement Categories are:

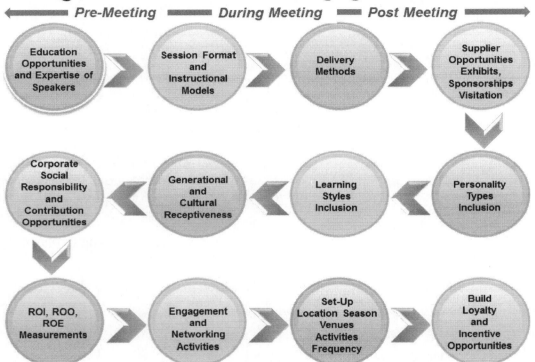

Meeting Effectiveness and Engagement Quotient©

⟵ Pre-Meeting ━━ During Meeting ━━ Post Meeting ⟶

Education Opportunities and Expertise of Speakers → Session Format and Instructional Models → Delivery Methods → Supplier Opportunities Exhibits, Sponsorships Visitation

Corporate Social Responsibility and Contribution Opportunities ← Generational and Cultural Receptiveness ← Learning Styles Inclusion ← Personality Types Inclusion

ROI, ROO, ROE Measurements → Engagement and Networking Activities → Set-Up Location Season Venues Activities Frequency → Build Loyalty and Incentive Opportunities

Meeting / event effectiveness and engagement quantifies the extent to which a desired outcome is achieved to meet or exceed the goals and objectives of the meeting. The Meeting Effectiveness and Engagement Quotient provides a roadmap to develop the targeted meeting / event content for the optimal experience and measures the attendees' experience in the pre-, during-, and post-meeting / event in 12 critical components. ©Debi Scholar. 2013

1. Education Opportunities and Expertise of Speakers / Instructors
2. Session Format and Instructional Models and Take-Away materials
3. Delivery Methods (face-to-face, virtual, hybrid, etc.)
4. Supplier Opportunities, Exhibits, Sponsorships, Visitation
5. Corporate Social Responsibility (CSR) and Contribution Opportunities
6. Generational and Cultural Receptiveness
7. Learning Styles Inclusion

8. Personality Types Inclusion
9. ROI, ROO, ROE Measurements
10. Engagement and Networking Activities
11. Set-Up, Location, Seasons of Event, Venues, Activities, Frequency
12. Build Loyalty and Incentive Opportunities

An example of the Meeting Effectiveness and Engagement Quotient Scorecard for a past meeting is illustrated in Figure 1. The actual scorecard is more detailed; this example is simplified for this book. Debi provides an in-depth analysis into each of the 12 categories with clients to measure their current meeting effectiveness and engagement and then we construct a plan for their upcoming meetings, events, and conferences to ensure that Meeting Effectiveness and Engagement provides the attendee with the feeling, "That was a GREAT meeting!"

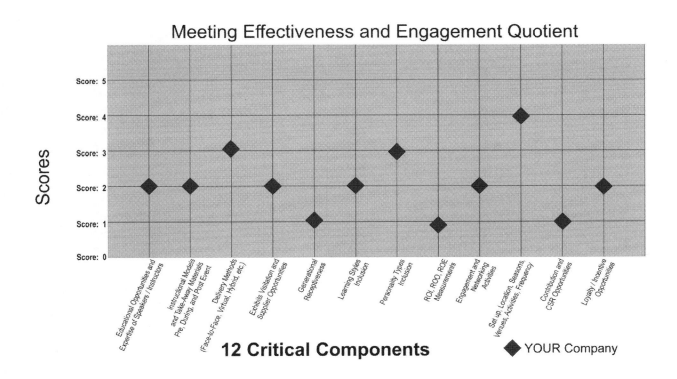

Please reach out to Debi if you would like to evaluate your Meeting Effectiveness and Engagement Quotient.©

Meeting Types

Based on the meeting type, it may require different kinds of hotels or unique venues.

This information will help you understand the meeting needs and guide your search for the right type of property.

You may also want to offer virtual meeting options to replace or complement some types of meetings.

You should be aware that many organizations require their meeting requesters and budget holders to consider whether the meeting is absolutely necessary and whether the content could be delivered by other means. Some organizations state that in-person meetings should occur only when there is a significant value added to the business that cannot be accomplished through teleconferencing, videoconferencing or web-based tools.

Many organizations require that their meetings be held at an office location, which is the "business norm," and that meetings held outside of the office are only allowable when internal space is not available.

- What type of meeting is it?
  For example:
  - Breakfast, lunch or dinner gatherings
  - Client / sales meetings or events
  - Incentive meetings or events
  - Marketing meetings or events
  - Sponsorship activities
  - Recruiting meetings or events
  - Special events / team outings
  - General business meetings
  - Project team meetings / events
  - Training meetings
  - Conferences or congresses
  - Virtual meetings held on-site or off-site that include 100 or more attendees and are not self-service.

In addition, when meetings are held in the office, it is usually a best practice and a requirement to use the in-house, contracted catering services that provide breakfasts / lunches where available. This additional revenue for the supplier helps reduce the overall costs for the staff and the organization.

Notes

Internal Conference Room Contacts

Processes to Reserve Internal Rooms

Attendees

Identify your attendees so that you can get a good sense as to how many people will be attending your meeting. If you understand the target audience or attendees, it will help you provide the right level of services and identify the appropriate hotel / venue.

Some meetings may be held locally and room nights may not be needed. For some meetings, only some of the attendees need room reservations.

Determine if any of the attendees will need to share rooms (double-double room type) or have a single room (queen or king room type).

If you are building an attendee registration website, you will need to accumulate all of the attendee data in an Excel file or some other preferred method so that the meeting website can be built and invitations can be sent. In an ideal world, you will gather this information and import it into your meeting management technology so that your attendees will be able to register by using a professional website.

- Who are the Attendees?

  For example:

  - Associates
  - Senior Associates
  - Managers
  - Vice Presidents / Senior Leaders
  - External clients and perspective clients
  - Support staff to ensure meeting success (e.g., IT professionals, on-site support, etc.)
  - Facilitators, trainers, speakers, etc.

- Is the meeting / event "open" or "invitation only?"
- How many attendees are expected?
- How many attendees will require room nights?
  - What nights will sleeping rooms be required?
  - How many sleeping rooms will be required each night?
  - How will needs for early arrival / late departures be covered?
  - Will attendees be required to share rooms?
  - Will any suites be needed for any speakers or VIPs?
- Will attendees make their own reservation directly with the hotel or will you collect the RSVPs and provide a rooming list to the hotel?

Example of a template that can be used to identify where the attendees originate from:

	First Name	Last Name	Level (e.g., associate, manager, vice president, etc.)	Title (e.g., Human Resources Director)	Company	City of Origin	Internal or External to the organization	Role at the meeting (e.g., attendee, support staff, speaker)	Email Address (to send invitation)
1.	Susan	Losurdo	Manager	Marketing Manager	ABC Company	Greenville, NC	Internal	Attendee	salosurdo @ gmail.com
2.	Debi	Scholar	Associate	Training Associate	ABC Company	Scotch Plains, NJ	Internal	Training Facilitation	debi@ debischolar. com

Meeting Date, Checklist, and Timeline

When you have flexibility in your dates, you will have the best opportunity to negotiate the best rates. Most hotels have less expensive days of the week so if cost is an issue, then be flexible in the days of the week you need the meeting. Similarly, cities and properties usually have seasons that are more costly.

When a meeting request is initiated, you must react quickly to not miss a key requirement and to obtain best pricing.

Advance planning is advantageous to both the meeting requester and you.

- When do you want to hold the meeting?
- Do you have a second choice of dates?
- How many days is your meeting?
- What are the preferred days of the week, month, and year of the meeting? Information requested (month, year, preferred days of the week).
- What is the lead-time before the meeting?

The following is an example of recommended lead times but many planners use different variations.

Approximate Value in US$	Average Attendees	Average Requested Lead Time (days)
Small meeting up to $10K	11 – 30	30 – 60
$10K to $20K	30 – 60	45 – 90
$20K to $40K	60 – 90	90 – 120
$40K to $80K*	90 – 120	120 – 160
$80K to $200K*	120 – 175	160 – 180
Over $200K*	175 – 350	180 – 240
*Note that anything that is estimated to cost over $50K should be planned 12–18 months in advance to leverage negotiating power and to ensure that the meeting is placed on the organization's and staff's meeting calendar.		

Checklists

Create a timeline from the date of the meeting working backwards. For example, below is a basic timeline. Many of these types of timelines can also be found online. See the Appendix for a sample meeting planning checklist to enhance your timeline.

Basic Planning Timeline for Small to Mid-Size meetings

4-6 Months Before Meeting

- Identify the purpose and objectives of the meeting; determine if there will be a meeting "theme"
- Develop the budget; review past meetings for historic spend information
- Identify the location and venues; send out RFPs, select and contract with venue (using professional legal review or review by a professional meeting planner)
- Identify speakers, ground transportation supplier, entertainment, and offsite activities
- Develop preliminary agenda
- Identity resources who can help you and prepare them for upcoming tasks that will need to be accomplished
- Identify # of attendees and begin collecting information on who the attendees are (e.g. name, phone, email, etc.)
- Determine if your meeting will use a mobile application; if yes, select supplier and begin development
- Identify ways to promote the meeting, if applicable

2-3 Months Before Meeting

- Finalize agenda
- Develop the meeting registration website (agenda, venue, transportation information, activity selection, etc.)
- Send invitations or at a minimum, a "save the date;" determine the deadline for registering for the meeting but ensure that it is well in advance before the hotel cut off date
- Confirm speakers, meeting specifications (room set up), food and beverage, audio-visual, technology,
- Develop crisis management plans (see "Crisis Management Handbook: A Quick Reference Guide for Meeting Planners")
- Order gifts or giveaways
- Pay deposits that may be required

1-2 Months Before Meeting

- Secure Certificates of Insurance for activities that may not be covered
- Ensure that all contracts (hotel, audio-visual, offsite activities, caterers, etc.) are signed and countersigned.
- Continually update the budget as necessary, but never deleting the original budget; rather, show the budget progression as the meeting progresses
- Identify # of attendees and begin collecting information on who the attendees are (e.g. name, phone, email, etc.)

- Confirm that you have provided all details to the speakers, PowerPoint templates if applicable, travel arrangements for speakers, and ask for their audio-visual needs

- Finalize menus and room set-ups with the hotel and offsite caterers

- Finalize entertainment, offsite activities, and décor if applicable

- Start developing collateral (brochures, registration kits, name badges, etc.)

- Obtain signage as necessary for each room (foam core boards, or communicate to the hotel the exact posting for each meeting room)

1 Month Before Meeting

- Confirm attendee lists

- Provide the attendee travel information (manifests) to the ground transportation company so that they know when to pick up each traveler from the airport. (via SUVs, sedans, mini-coaches, etc.)

- Confirm rooming lists and be sure to tell the hotel who should get the upgrades, e.g. suite

3 Weeks Before Meeting

- Finalize meeting specifications (room set-ups, food & beverage plans, etc.)

2 Weeks Before Meeting

- Finalize collateral, name badges, etc. Recognize that there will always be last minute changes onsite or the day before

- If you are using seating charts, prepare them. This may be for your seating at meeting tables or even at meals

- Send emails to all parties as necessary

  ➤ Remind speakers who will pick them up from airport, where they are staying, rehearsal information, what time they need to be in whatever room they are speaking in, what time they may depart from hotel, where to find car to take them back to airport, how to get reimbursed for expenses, who to contact if they cannot locate their ground transportation service, who to contact in case of emergency, etc.

  ➤ May want to provide your attendees with their registration confirmation and a memo with all final details

  ➤ May want to call or email all suppliers to ensure they do not have any questions and that everything is ready to go.

  ➤ May want to provide your support staff with information about their roles onsite

- Have boxes shipped to Hotel to arrive 1-2 days before meeting

- Arrange for the guestroom deliveries of gifts or meeting materials for all or partial attendees as applicable. For example, you may want to arrange with the hotel to have information / gifts placed in sleeping rooms on the day of arrival

- Reconfirm rooming lists with hotel if this is the final cut-off date (see hotel contract for actual date.)
- Obtain travel manifests from travel company to arrange ground transportation pick-up from airport and the return ground transportation back to the airport

3 Working Days Prior to Meeting

- Confirm food and beverage guarantees with hotel

Day Before Meeting

- Run through your checklist and confirm that nothing is missing
- Plan for gratuities (e.g. how you will pay, etc. See On-Site section for more information)
- Set up office and registration desk (if space permits)
- Arrive at hotel to check facility, rooms, boxes that may have been shipped, where restrooms are located, etc.
- Assemble materials
- Check signage
- Rehearsals
- Monitor arrivals and departures
- VIP Meet and Greets
- Suite checks
- Amenity deliveries
- Ensure that your Crisis Management Plans, meeting information, and important phone numbers are in your binder ready to go (or on your iPad / tablet). Note: hard copies are always handy in case of a crisis where electricity may not be available.
- If your meeting starts early the next day, it is wise to meet your hotel staff that will be supporting your event on the day before (called a "pre-con", for pre-conference meeting) Go over all of the details with these staff members to make sure everyone understands all of the requirements.
- Meet and brief internal staff and other suppliers

Day of Meeting

- Read: "On-site at Meeting" section of this Playbook
- Bring your binder, checklists, cell phone charger and whatever else you need
- Arrive early, possibly by 6:00 a.m. or 6:30 a.m. to check on breakfast
- If you did not meet the hotel staff yesterday, meet them today and be sure that everyone has an understanding of the meeting agenda and what is required. Get their names and cell phone numbers.

- Print attendee lists alphabetically (and by table if seating is assigned) and have it ready at the registration desk with the name badges.

- Bring extra blank name badges

- Request and review hotel reports

- Set materials and supplies in each meeting room

- If you have assigned seating, set up the name tents / tent cards according to seating charts

- Check meeting rooms to confirm they are set correctly

- Connect with speakers and VIPs

- Continuously check food and beverage services

- Monitor agenda for break times and attendee movement

- Secure rooms while meetings are not in session

- Review hotel invoices from previous days

- Distribute evaluations (paper or technology-based). Note that some organizations send evaluations out a few days after the meeting if using technology

At Meetings End:

- Collect completed meeting evaluations

- Collect and dispose of confidential materials

- Pack and ship any leftover materials, supplies, items, etc.

- Distribute hotel gratuities and thank you notes

- Monitor hotel Check Out

- Manage departures

- Conduct preliminary bill review with the hotel to discuss all charges incurred to date

- Conduct a "post-con" (post-conference meeting) with hotel director to discuss service levels

After the Meeting

- Conduct Meeting / Event Sponsor Debrief

- Review all of the invoices and dispute the charges immediately that you do not believe are correct

- Pay the invoices

- Report metrics (forecasted budget vs. actual, and other metrics that are recommended in this Playbook)

- Write thank yous

Notes

Additional items to add to my timeline

Meeting Location

When you have flexibility in your locations, you will have the best opportunity to negotiate the best rates. It is a good practice to have a sense as to where your attendees originate from so that you can select the most central and / or the most cost-effective location for your meeting. For example, if most of the attendees are in the Northeast, it may not make sense to transport the majority to Florida when there are cost-effective cities in the Northeast to hold your meeting, unless of course, the goal of the meeting supports the destination chosen.

Some organizations require that the meeting be held at a site that minimizes travel and overnight accommodations when most attendees are from the same location. You may want to ask your preferred travel management company to provide you with an air fare analysis to help you select the most cost-effective location based on where the majority of attendees originate.

Weigh your best options based on the seasons, cost and locations. Sometimes, a secondary city (Nashville, St. Louis, Milwaukee rather than NYC, LA or Chicago) may be the best choice.

- Where do you want to hold the meeting? Information requested:
  - Region, city, state
  - Central location
- Where are the attendees coming from?
  - Are all attendees local (able to drive in?)
  - Are attendees regional (limited need for air travel?)
  - Are attendees situated across the country or the world (most requiring air travel?)
- Are there hotels or venues to which you would like to send a request for proposal?
- Is it possible to consider using a facility that offers a Complete Meeting Package (CMP) rate which is all-inclusive and usually, less costly than a hotel?
- Are there penalty credits available for use?

It is a good idea to send out a minimum of three request for proposals to hotels so that you can identify the best and most cost-effective location. In addition, when you send out the request for proposals to three properties, it reduces your risk exposure because you are giving suppliers a fair opportunity to bid on your meeting and you are evaluating the responses fairly, which are requirements of procurement organizations and aligned with Sarbanes-Oxley guidelines.

When you contact a hotel, the Hotel Sales Department will work with you to discuss your dates for the meeting, the space you may need (meeting rooms, sleeping rooms, room for breakfast / lunch, etc.), the rates you can expect to pay, and the services you need.

Penalties may have been incurred by your organization from other meeting cancellations or attrition fees (when the contracted attendance was not fulfilled). If there are penalty credits available for use at hotel properties, it would be wise to use them so that the money is not left on the table and unused. Speak with your professional meeting planners, or if you do not have professional meeting planners at your organization, ask your hotel properties if there are any credits outstanding that you can use.

Facilities that offer Complete Meeting Package (CMP) rates are often less expensive than hotels when you consider expenses for food, beverages, meeting space, sleeping rooms and audio-visual equipment. Even though meeting space may be complimentary at a hotel, conference center CMP rates are all-inclusive prices and often less expensive.

When you narrow down the venues, you may want to schedule a site visit with the property, preferably with the professional meeting planner as he / she will know exactly what to ask and look for in a property. Site visits allow you to review the venue, meet the staff, evaluate the destination, see the meeting space and sleeping rooms, taste the food, and analyze the environment (e.g. parking, restaurants, etc.). Many site inspection checklists are available online.

Budgets

Planning the budget for a meeting / event is not an easy task. If you have budget information on similar, historic meetings that were held, the data will help you create a budget for your current meeting or event. For starters, consider the cost of the guest rooms, food and beverage, the meeting costs, air and ground transportation, content costs, printing and collateral costs, and shipping costs.

While some planners share their budgets upfront with their suppliers, the author recommends keeping your budget confidential and to not share it with your suppliers. Of course, you can provide your suppliers with a range, but why give away the bank? Rather, ask hotels and other suppliers for their costs based on your needs and then begin negotiating the prices based on what the suppliers provide to you. In addition, this is usually the model that procurement organizations prefer too. Of course, if you only have $100 per person to spend on a dinner but you know you need a cocktail reception, open bar, and four course meal, then it is best to share the budget in advance with the caterer so that they can prepare a proposal for you within your range. Work with your professional meeting planners to estimate the meeting costs and identify where and when negotiations will be effective. Another option is to use the meeting management technology calculators to estimate your meeting budget.

Based on industry averages, a typical meeting requires three contracts (one for the hotel property, one for ancillary services such as audio-visual, and one for ground transportation or other services).

- What is the budget?
- Will you be paying for everything? Or only partial expenses if attendees are contributing?
- Do you have historic data from previous, similar meetings that you can use?
- Do you have a meeting management technology system that you can use to create and store the budget?
- Have you considered the costs of the:
  - Venue / hotel sleeping rooms and room rental (if applicable)
  - Content
  - Transportation (air, ground)
  - Audio-visual, technology
  - Food and beverage service
  - Entertainment
  - Décor
  - Gifts
  - Alcohol
  - Shipping
  - Print materials
  - Security
  - On-site support
  - Tax / gratuities
- What form of payment will be used?
- Are deposits required?
- Do we need to fill out a direct bill application?
- Will the room and tax be billed to a master account or will each attendee be required to pay for their own expenses?
- Will the attendees be required to submit a Travel and Entertainment Expense report for the meeting expenses?

The Appendix provides you with a sample template that you may use to estimate your budget. It is important to keep track of your itemized forecasted budget, your itemized actual expenses. and the difference between the two. Raise questions and concerns to your budget holders immediately should cost exceed the budgeted amount.

Establish a form of payment for the meeting services and suppliers. You may want to use a credit card such as a procurement card or meetings card. Usually, it is not advisable to use a corporate card because the corporate card holder may accumulate points which costs the organization more money; and this arrangement may be deemed unethical in some organizations. The entire event can be paid for on a purchasing card or meeting card, or you may elect to have a portion of the meeting paid by the attendee. In addition, you can always use the invoice / accounts payable method; however, the data-rich information gained by using the card will be lost. In addition, it takes many days, even months, to get checks approved in some organizations; your suppliers may not want to wait for a check. The National Association for Purchase Card Professionals, also known as the Professional Association for the Commercial Card and Payment Industry, has stated that approximately $63, per transaction, can be saved in processing costs by using a card vs. a check request.

In a spend analysis at one organization, it was uncovered that some managers were dividing the costs of their meetings among numerous General Ledger and Budget codes so that the total cost of their meetings were under the threshold of review. Yet, the total costs of their meetings were significantly more than the leaders expected.

Meeting costs include air, rail, hotel, restaurants, ground, audio-visual, entertainment, destination management companies, meeting planning companies, speakers, team building, printing, shipping, production companies, tickets and ticket brokers, bleacher rentals, and the list continues.

As a result, this organization required that all meetings be registered in one central repository with budget codes and general ledger numbers assigned to each category of spend per business unit.

Agenda

Your daily agenda will be the basis for many decisions. The timed agenda will help you determine if the following are needed:

- Number of meeting rooms and the sizes needed (e.g., general session and breakout rooms)

- Room setup (e.g., theatre, classroom, boardroom, banquet, crescent rounds, u-shape, etc.) See the Appendix for sampler room set-ups.

- Coffee break schedule

- Registration desk

- Separate rooms for food and beverage

- On-site office equipped with telephones, fax, copier, computers and office supplies

- Off-site activities

- Graphic design and print distribution services (invitations, agendas, brochures, etc.) Content development assistance /facilitation /speaker / training requirements

- What is the proposed daily agenda?
  - Registration
  - General session
  - Breakouts
  - Meals
  - Breaks
  - Social activities
  - Evening events
  - Other
- How many days is your meeting / event?
- Will the attendees all be arriving on the same day or different days?
- What type of activities would you like to include?

If your activities are held off-site, then this information can be determined after the hotel contract is signed. However, if you require special activities that will affect the cost of the hotel contract, then it is important to discuss these activities before signing the hotel contract.

Many activities such as teambuilding and off-site dining events are easily managed by professional meeting planners. Yet some activities pose a higher risk and may require additional insurance. For example, boat rides, parasailing, rock climbing, helicopter rides, hot air balloons and mechanical bull riding may be more risky. These activities are not usually covered under the organization's liability insurance and may require individual releases, waivers of liability, or separate certifications of insurance. Be sure to ask your professional meeting planners, your risk / compliance department, or your insurance specialists to help you obtain the proper approvals and insurance so that your organization does not incur significant liability.

For example, the following may be a method to segregate your activities:

Approved activities without additional insurance or intervention	Activities that require additional insurance	Activities that are NEVER allowed
Cooking classes	Boating excursions (notify for all types of boats)	Riding an electronic bull
Golf	Horseback riding	Wave runners or jet skis
Tennis	Rock climbing	Surfing
Spa	Scuba diving	ATV riding
Tours	Trap / skeet shooting	Bungee jumping
Go karts	Zip line	Parachuting / parasailing
Kayaking	Roller coasters on top of tall towers	Hang-gliding
Land rover or jeep rides	Charity work / volunteering (e.g., Habitat for Humanity)	Helicopter rides
Falconry	Motor speedway rides	Motorcycle or scooter riding
Snorkeling	Deep sea fishing	Glider rides
Bicycling – mountain or otherwise	Hot air ballooning	
Hiking		
Fencing		
Exercise (Tai Chi, Pilates, aerobics)		

Of course, entertainment activities should never occur at gentlemen's clubs (or like establishments), or venues that do not reflect a professional atmosphere.

Always consider the American with Disabilities Act (ADA) and ensure that activities are appropriate.

If you want to play music at your meeting / event, you cannot play licensed music unless you obtain a license to do so from either BMI or ASCAP. Your entertainment providers (Musicians, Bands, DJ) must typically carry the appropriate licensing. However, every time Debi has asked the suppliers to see their music license, they cannot provide a copy of it. So, ASK to see their license. If they do not carry it, it is your organization's responsibility to obtain the license. For more information about music licensing for your meeting or event, see these resources:

http://www.ascap.com/licensing/types/conventions-expos-trade-shows.aspx

http://www.bmi.com/licensing/

Notes
Contact information to obtain Certificates of Insurance
Contact information to obtain BMI / ASCAP License

Suppliers and Contracts

Selecting a Venue

It is important to select the right type of venue that matches the goals of your meeting / event. For example, a training program or board meeting may fit well into a hotel meeting room whereas a unique reception could be placed in a hotel ballroom or lounge area, or, it could also be placed in a nice museum or unique venue. While some companies allow meetings to be held in gaming cities (e.g. Las Vegas, Atlantic City) and may have an off-site activity in a casino to watch a show, other companies will not place any meetings in those cities. Of course, we have nothing against these cities, but it is important to understand the culture of the organization and the goals of the meeting.

When searching for a venue, consider the dates, rates, space, and service. Below are some of the questions that may need answers:

Dates

- Does the venue have the dates you need for your meeting / event?
- Are there less expensive dates?
- What else is occurring in the venue, area, and city over these dates?
- Did we check the global holiday calendar to reduce conflicts?
- Did we check to see if competitors are conducting meetings at the venue?

Rates

- What factors will we use to evaluate the venues?
- What are the costs of each component of the meeting or event?

Space

- What is the room / space you need based on the room layout you have selected? For a room size calculator, visit this website: http://www.cvent.com/rfp/SpaceCalculatorPopup.htm
- Do you need break-out session rooms? Do you need additional space for meals?
- What type of equipment do you need in the space, such as podium, AV, sound, lighting?
- Does the space have obstructions that could cause issues during your meeting or during the breaks while people are moving to and from other areas?
- Are you able to hold your space overnight?

Service

- Do you have any special services needed for your meeting? For example, the services offered in a 3-star rated property are different from a 5-star rated property.
- Do you have any onsite activities you may want to experience, such as onsite spa, nearby golf courses?

Evaluation Chart

Use an Evaluation Chart (sometimes called a Scorecard) to evaluate the venues. The Evaluation Chart below should have more columns for considerations such as:

- Dates and Times Available
- Liquor License or Beer / Wine only
- AV, Microphone, Podium allowances
- Deposit required
- Attendee count cut-off date
- And, there may be more columns that you will need to evaluate your options

Sample Evaluation Chart for Evening Event					
Venue	Room Rental for Event	Food and Beverage Estimated Cost	Space Available	Proximity to Transportation (air, train)	Special Considerations
Hotel #1	$5,000	$33,500	Outdoor Courtyard	3 blocks	Due to noise restriction, must end by 10:00 pm
Hotel #2	Waived	$36,200	Private Dining Room	5 miles	Because dining room is near public area, no microphones are allowed for speeches, etc.
Restaurant	Waived	$35,000	Private Dining Room	1 mile	Only available from 7:00 pm to 11:00 pm
Museum	$2,500	$31,000	Entire first floor	5 blocks	Catering Service must own liquor license as museum does not have it

Paying for a Venue

You will need to submit a Direct Bill Application to the hotel. A company needs to be approved for direct billing before a master account can be set up. If your company does not have adequate credit, then the venue will require a significant deposit or even full prepayment. Direct Bill Applications can take up to 30 days to be processed so this should be addressed during the contract stage. A best practice is to use a Meeting Card or Procurement Card to pay for your meeting /event instead of a check.

Selecting suppliers fairly

Many organizations have ethical policies on obtaining and using complimentary rooms or services, personal incentive points, tickets, credits, gifts or other awards that may be offered by suppliers. Some organizations state that any points or credits that may be earned through a meeting may not be credited to an individual meeting host, budget holder or meeting planner and must be used to benefit the organization's business activities. (Note that this does not include the individual point programs offered by hotels, airlines, and credit card companies).

Selecting suppliers fairly is a good business practice and usually accomplished through request for proposals and evaluation scorecards.

> - What ethical practices should be followed?
> - How are suppliers selected?
> - Is a site visit to the property or venue needed?
> - Are meeting planner points collected? And, if so, how are they used?
> - Should we consider using suppliers that are registered as a diverse? E.g. minority owned, woman-owned, etc.
> - Should we consider using a supplier who supports our green meeting efforts?

> In one organization, a leader requested complimentary services from a hotel for holding a large, annual meeting at their property. For the first couple of years, meeting planners were reticent about bringing this unethical behavior forward. After the organization encouraged people to step forward with unethical behaviors, one person revealed that these requests were made of the hotel.

While we discuss hotels for the most part in this Playbook, this practice of using request for proposals and selecting suppliers fairly is applicable for any type of vendor.

Most important it may be deemed unethical to consistently award business to one supplier without a thorough review of the marketplace, especially if that supplier is a friend or relative.

> In one organization, it was uncovered that numerous meeting planners were collecting and keeping hotel meeting planner points for their personal use. When the organization learned of this behavior, it reached out to each hotel chain to obtain the value of the points, and required that each meeting planner pay back the amount to the organization.

Preparing to sign the contract

When hotels hold space for a meeting, it is expected that a contract will be signed by both your organization and the hotel.

Negotiating with a venue can be a very complex process, as there are so many factors to consider. It is strongly recommended that a professional meeting planner conduct the negotiations with the suppliers. Based on the number of sleeping rooms required, the meeting space may be complimentary as well as numerous other concessions (items that are discounted or complimentary). Professional meeting planners will negotiate rates, services, amenities, concessions, attrition / cancellation penalties, dates, space requirements, signage, audio-visual, resources on-site, and which companies may be allowed at the facility at the same time as your organization. Surely, you do not want your organization's competitors on the property at the same time as you are there. It is also important to track all of the savings that have been negotiated with the hotel or other suppliers so that you can report that information to the meeting requester or budget holder.

- Are you prepared to commit to signing a contract to hold the meeting?
- Has someone from your legal or procurement department reviewed the contract?
- Who from your organization is allowed to sign a hotel or other type of contract?
- Are you prepared to commit to an accurate number of attendees?

Debi has created an addendum with key terms and concessions that you will want to include in your hotel contract. Although we have included sample room attrition and cancellation grids in the Appendix, the contract information can be found online at Debi's blog. We added the attrition and cancellation grids because this information is so important to calculate for your hotel contracts. Ask a hotel to clearly define how much you will owe on the exact date should your attendance fall short of the commitment or if you cancel your meeting. Remember, these terms are negotiable. For more information on hotel contracts, visit www.TEPlus.net.

A hotel's revenue management leaders will not allow the sales staff to hold space without a contract if other buyers are interested in their space.

In a more stressed economy, the hotels were more likely to hold space as meeting volume declined. However, with the market and economy improvement, buyers are contracting with hotels quickly so they do not lose space.

Many organizations allow only designated leaders to sign contracts that commit the organization to financial liability. Make sure that you ask your leaders and / or the professional meeting planners who can sign the contracts on behalf of the organization. In addition, many organizations do not allow third-party providers to sign contracts on their behalf.

> In one organization, they held an offsite activity at an outdoor activity center. Thankfully, the meeting planner added the right terms and conditions because a wind storm blew a heavy table into one of the attendees. As the attendee was headed into the ambulance, the activity center tried to obtain a signature from him confirming that they were not responsible. However, the proper language was already in the contract holding the facility liable.

Notes

**People allowed to sign Hotel Contracts
(e.g. Managers, VPs, Procurement, Legal, etc.)**

Name, Email, and Phone Number

Name, Email, and Phone Number

Familiarization Trips / Complimentary Services

It is industry standard for hotel companies and meeting vendors to extend invitations for meals or familiarization trips to organization staff. Acceptance of luncheon, reception or activity (golf tournament, sports events, etc.) invitations should be discussed and approved in advance with the staff members' respective manager or the procurement organization.

Many organizations do not accept any form of trips or complimentary services at all. And, this is usually a wise, ethical practice.

Some organizations allow a meeting planner to accept an invitation to a Familiarization Trip only under the following conditions:

- When there is a legitimate business case for attending
- Approval in advance by the department manager and procurement manager
- Time and expenses chargeable to the organization for the trip are estimated and approved in advance by the department manager and procurement manager (It may be better that the organization pay a fee to the host to cover costs and avoid issues of impropriety)
- A post meeting site report is reported back to the staff member's supervisor

Some organizations require that luncheons, receptions or gifts must be reported on a quarterly basis by completing a form and sending a copy to the department manager.

Thinking Ahead: Policies, Exceptions, and Reporting

It is much easier to proactively identify meeting policy or rules that should be followed and communicate these expectations to the attendees rather than manage reactively to attendees' requests. For example, attendees may want to know if they are allowed to travel by business class or first class seating. Another example will be to provide answers to those attendees who may question if they have to share rooms. In fact, many companies still require attendees to share rooms to save costs. While many companies may require lower level staff to share rooms, the author knows of one company that still requires its senior level staff to share rooms. And, even the CEO has shared his room on occasion to save the organization money. These types of policies should be communicated proactively.

- Are there policies or rules that should be followed?
- How are exceptions going to be handled?
- What type of data metrics and reports will you need?

Also, questions will arise throughout the planning stages so identify who will answer attendees' questions and provide approvals on exceptions requested. For example, an attendee may want to arrive early, stay longer, stay with a relative, etc. These types of questions should have canned answers ready to go.

Identify the data and metrics reporting requirements before the meeting / event is planned and held so that you can obtain the statistics required to calculate the value and return on investment. Examples of metrics that you may want to capture are in the Reporting, Debriefs, and Thank You chapter of the this book.

Notes

Policy requirements to remember:

Frequently Asked Questions List:

Person to approve exceptions (name, email and phone)

Data we may want to collect after meeting

Technology Options

Meeting Management Technologies

Many organizations use a licensed, web-based meeting technology to manage the end-to-end meeting sourcing and planning process.

Few meeting management technology companies offer end-to-end strategic meetings management functionality as well as meeting planning functionality. A meeting management technology should offer the functionality that a planner needs as well as what the director wants in order to oversee the whole meeting / event program.

- What type of technology will facilitate the meeting sourcing and planning process?
- What functionality does the meeting technology offer?
- Do we need a mobile application?
- Do we need an Audience Response System (ARS)?

Consider the following list of functionality requirements for your meeting management technology:

- Forecast meetings by registering everything into an enterprise-wide online calendar system
- Resource management of team members assigned to work on the meeting
- eRFPs to search for and source hotels and other suppliers
- Contract / document management to retain information in one system accordingly
- Central location for meeting policy, FAQs, budget calculators, processes, etc.
- Approval routing of meetings to ensure that leaders sign-off on meetings
- Database of suppliers to search for hotels, venues, and other vendors (e.g. audio-visual)
- Attendee management / rooming lists, etc.
- Communications / RSVPs
- Survey / return on investment
- Payment and reconciliation (payment to suppliers; accept payments from attendees; payment to speakers, etc.)
- Enterprise-wide data reporting (across all meetings, all sourcing, all attendees, all surveys, etc.)
- Compliance tracking if applicable
- Multiple language capabilities
- Ability to integrate seamlessly with Customer Relationship Management (CRM), Online Booking Tool (OBT), Enterprise Resource Planning (ERP), Enterprise Contract Management (ECM), Learning Management System (LMS), compliance databases, etc.

Meeting Management Technologies (e.g. StarCite, Cvent, Lenos, Arcaneo Metron, SignUp4) can provide numerous benefits by automating many tasks.

In one organization, the meeting planner used Excel to create the attendee list which included names, credit card information, and attendees' special requirements. Unfortunately, the computer was stolen which exposed the organization to the loss of Personal Identifiable Information. As a result, the organization was fined.

Audience Response Systems

An Audience Response System (ARS) is both a term used, and a technology system, used to create interactivity between the audience and the presenter(s). Both a hardware requirement (handheld device, Smartphone, iPad, etc.) and presentation software integrate to offer audience engagement. Contact SmartSource Computer and Audio Visual.

Mobile Applications

Mobile applications provide improved attendee experiences, processes, and efficiency by combining a great deal of information compacted into a mobile application. For example, a meeting agenda, program, maps, sponsors, exhibits, photos and social media can all be incorporated into a mobile application. Determine the functionality, support, and connectivity options needed. For example, one of the big considerations is whether or not the mobile application needs connection to the Internet to function properly. Unfortunately, many hotels do not have strong cell phone connections in the interiors of their properties leading to dysfunction of the mobile application. To reduce these risks, it may be better to consider a "native" application, or an application that resides on the Smartphone or tablet device so that you can be sure it works. Crowd Compass is one mobile application that offers this functionality.

iPads

iPads are becoming more of a standard to deliver content and become the device of choice for many meeting presenters. A provisioned iPad (an iPad that includes pre-loaded materials with a uniform interface) provides the equipment and solution for effective and powerful content delivery without the risk exposure of Bring Your Own Device (BYOD). If organizations allow BYOD for delivery of meeting content, then data confidentiality, privacy, support, and metrics are unavailable. Moreover, attendees multi-task into other device applications. When presenters develop their content, they are held to the onerous PowerPoint rules: large type and up to six bulleted lines. To complement those presentations, your iPads can contain more complex data on an iPad screen that can be magnified so that your attendees get the right information, on the right-sized screen, at the right time. For more information on using provisioned iPads for your meetings, contact SmartSource Computer and Audio Visual.

RFID

Radio-Frequency Identification (RFID) is very useful when embedded in name badges. RFID technology allows you to track and securely manage attendee information for attendance purposes.

Technology Connectivity

Attendees need to be able to connect to the Internet in this 24/7 economy and environment. The challenge is to create an environment of an "office away from the office" if the meeting requires it. It is very common for attendees to use a Blackberry for their work email and telephone calls, an iPhone for their personal email and telephone calls, an iPad, and a laptop. Do you need to prepare for at least three or four devices per attendee to be connected to the network at your meeting? Absolutely. A robust network is the norm and people expect it.

Moreover, hotels often offer basic or advanced connectivity. The advanced connectivity costs more but the success of your meeting may require it. If you do not plan for this critical connectivity component in advance, then your attendees will lose efficiency and effectiveness while onsite at your meeting.

To help you estimate the amount of network connectivity or bandwidth that you need at your event, APEX[3] has developed a "Bandwidth Estimator for Meetings and Events." Using this calculator, we input 50 attendees that required a high amount of bandwidth using multiple devices. The calculator estimates that we will require 11 Mb/s. With this information in hand, we can negotiate costs with our hotel or venue so that our attendees have the network connectivity they need while onsite at our meeting or event.

Bandwidth Estimator for Meetings and Events

Users(#): *   50

Must be a multiple of ten, up to 1000

Type: High   ▾

Low	Email and simple Web Surfing
Medium	Web Applications and Streaming Audio
High	Instructor Lead Web Training, Large File Transfers, SD Video Stream

Multiple devices: ☑

Check if most attendees will have multiple devices

Your Estimated Bandwidth

With **50 users**, using **multiple devices**, and **high** expected usage, we predict your required bandwidth to be approximately **11 Mb/s**.

---

3   Convention Industry Council, Accepted Practices Exchange

For more information about meeting / event bandwidth, please see these whitepapers:
http://www.conventionindustry.org/StandardsPractices/APEX/bandwidthconnectivity.aspx

To determine your network and support needs for the meeting, consider the following questions:

- How much bandwidth do we need? (See APEX Bandwidth Calculator Resource)
- What is best suited for your situation – wired or wireless?
- Is the bandwidth shared or dedicated?
- Will you need support staff to help attendees with connectivity, printing, software, hardware, devices, or other technology needs?
- Is there onsite IT support provided by the venue? What are their hours of coverage?
- Will your company's internal IT support staff want to conduct a pre-check of the network connectivity set-up at the hotel or venue?
- Will you include a technology lab, cyber café, device charging station, or other technology support area for your attendees?
- What type of network is in place at the hotel or venue? Will you use WiFi? Is the WiFi secure?
- Will network connectivity be in all meeting rooms, meeting offices, perimeter space, and sleeping rooms?
- How many IP addresses does the property supply? What is the lease time of the IP address?"
- Are there firewalls to be considered?
- What is the cost for connectivity? Routers? Network setup? Additional circuits / lines?

Consult with your internal IT specialists as well as hotel providers to ensure you have adequate technology operating at optimum levels.

Telecommunications

Dedicated outside phone lines may be needed in places like your office or registration to conduct operation. Cell phone service can be spotty in some hotel areas and cell phone battery life is limited.

Speakerphones are critical for conference calls.

Consider walkie talkie radios as a means of communication with hotel staff in order to have changes made quickly.

Communications

Frequently Asked Questions (FAQ)

It is wise to begin building a Frequently Asked Questions (FAQ) list during the pre-planning of the meeting so that as more questions arise, you have the answers to these questions.

> • What types of communications are needed with the:
>   - Attendees
>   - Suppliers
>   - Speakers / facilitators
>   - Support staff

Attendees

Save the Date

If you are sending out a "save the date" email, you may want to include information that informs recipients not to book air / ground transportation or hotel rooms until you provide them with the method to do so. See the Appendix for more information about registration communications.

Invitation / Registration

If you are building a registration website using the meeting technology, be prepared to include a welcome introduction, logo, agenda, air and ground transportation information including shuttle transfers, hotel/venue information, activity information and / or any other meeting details that you would like to have included on the website. It is always helpful for a website builder to develop the whole thing at once rather than in bits and pieces. Don't forget to answer all of the typical questions, Who, What, When, Where, Why, and How.

The type of information that you should collect from attendees regardless of how you get it, is:

- First name, last name (may want to ask if this is the preferred name for their name tag)
- Company name
- Title
- Phone number (preferred phone, mobile phone, may want FAX number)
- Email address
- Address (street, city, state/province, zip, country)
- Ask if they have any special physical or dietary needs
- Emergency contact information (name of person to contact, phone number, relationship to you)

See the Appendix for a sample Meeting Announcement and a Pre-Arrival Letter.

Suppliers

Communicate with suppliers before, during, and after the meeting. For example, your hotel, ground transportation, audio-visual, off-site activity(s), décor, and entertainment suppliers will need up-to-date information on location, the number of attendees, the agenda, the meeting flow, contact information, and what to do in case of a crisis or emergency.

Speakers / Facilitators

Communicate with speakers / facilitators as early and often as necessary to keep them informed. Provide them with the date, presentation time, location (city, facility, room number), date, meeting title, background on the company and / or meeting objective, local maps and facility layout. It is also important to communicate any rehearsal details. They may provide you with their session description, biography, and photo to input into your meeting program. Determine when you need their presentation but keep in mind that many presenters make changes to their presentation up until the minute before they go onstage (speaking from experience). Identify who will introduce the speaker.

Support Staff

Communicate with support staff (e.g. local administrative assistants, coordinators, etc.) that they are providing preplanning or onsite support to enhance the value of the meeting for the attendees. Support staff should not deem going onsite as a vacation or a means to get away from the office. Support staff are responsible to serve as role models and always carry themselves in a professional manner whether they are in the presence of attendees or not. Support staff may not be allowed to participate in the attendee meal functions or offsite activities, yet, of course are allowed to dine privately with other staff members. Support staff should be aware of all crisis management plans and follow those guidelines to help attendees or others as necessary. If invited to participate in bar / lounge activities, support staff may want to decline or only attend for a short period of time. Support staff should always make sure that their humor is fair and appropriate and immediately notify someone if an attendee uses humor or other language that may be inappropriate. Support staff often need to work long hours onsite such as 6:00 a.m. or 7:00 a.m. to the evening hours and may be asked to provide multiple services such as supporting the registration desk, copying, directing attendees to the right rooms, or performing other services.

Resources / Support Staff

Meetings require numerous skillsets such as negotiation, detailed planning, technology, and financial skillsets. While one person may be responsible to fulfill all of these requirements, often other people may be tasked to support the meeting planning activities. To that end, below is a template that you may want to use to identify resources who are available to assist throughout the meeting planning process.

- How many resources are required to support this meeting
- Where will the resources come from? (e.g., internal people, consultants, suppliers, or a hybrid approach of both)?

Resource Management			
Activity	**Insource**	**Outsource** (consultants / suppliers)	**Hybrid approach** (using both insourced and outsourced resources)
Project management: designing meeting content and logisticsz (sourcing, planning, on-site management)			
Site selection, sourcing, negotiation and contracting			
Planning logistics and ground transportation, overseeing air transportation			
Attendee management, communications, exceptions, rooming lists, RSVPs			
Meeting management, technology development and oversight			
Creative services (name tags, brochures, branding, marketing, etc.)			
On-site staffing (planners and hostesses)			
Meeting accountants (budget, invoices, dispute management, reconciliation)			
Value Added Tax (VAT) reclaim			

Resource Management			
Activity	**Insource**	**Outsource** (consultants / suppliers)	**Hybrid approach** (using both insourced and outsourced resources)
Data intelligence administrator (create and analyze reports)			
Production Coordination			
IT Support			
Security Staff			
Administrative Support			

Many organizations use support staff to help plan their meetings. Maybe you have supported other meetings and enjoyed the work! Regardless, if you are looking for more support staff to help you, below is a sample communication that you may want to consider using to recruit more staff that have mentioned the desire to work on meetings or events.

Communication to potential support staff:

Thank you for your interest in helping Meeting & Event Services onsite for upcoming meetings, events and programs. Assisting onsite requires **SHARPP** people!

- **S**aying YES to any task required
- **H**aving a positive attitude
- **A**vailability during multiple days and long, extended hours
- **R**eliability in attendance
- **P**atience with all levels of staff, partners, guests and team members
- **P**rofessionalism in communications, appearance and behavior

Roles onsite may include but are not limited to:

- Putting together the welcome packets
- Making nametags
- Making photocopies
- Answering phones, taking and posting messages
- Sending and receiving faxes
- Checking lists
- Taking requests
- Taking things to the business center to be shipped
- Helping with transportation changes

- Answering questions - many questions
- Assisting with registration
- Closing down the office on Sunday

If asked to go onsite, you will always require your computer and power cord. Sometimes onsite assistance requires a certain dress code such as matching shirts. If so, you will be provided with that attire. Please note that it is not acceptable to bring family members for your role onsite. Many times onsite staff do not have the opportunity to tour the local city so if that objective is driving your decision to volunteer, take a vacation to the area instead.

So that we have a current list of people to call upon for upcoming meetings, please complete the following information and return it to **[name]** by **[date]**. Please note that we may contact the person you've listed below as a "Recommendation Contact" as well as human resources for approval.

Name	
Role and Level within organization	
Work office location and phone	
Manager contact	
Number of people currently supported (that you have to answer to each day)	
Years with organization	
Referred by	
Recommendation contact	
Approval contact	
Backfill plans while out	
Previous onsite experience within the firm - if yes, please list	
Specific dates throughout 20XX that not available	
Why are you interested in helping Meeting & Event Services onsite?	

Meeting Specifications

After the hotel contract has been signed, your meeting will be turned over from your sales contact to a Convention Services Manager (CSM). The CSM will be your primary contact from this point forward.

Prepare detailed specifications that define all of your meeting needs, as it will be provided to the hotel. Some organizations use this document as an addendum to the contract. Other organizations may put some of the language directly into a master agreement or contract addendum and keep the specifications separate. Below is one example of a list of meeting specifications that lists the dates and rooming requirements needed. Be prepared with as much information as possible.

> * Who will be the hotel contact after we negotiate the contract? Who will be the Conference Services Manager?
> * How will I know what meeting rooms I have been assigned or that I selected?
> * What else should I tell the hotel, or should they be asking me?
> * Are we confident of the room set-up? (see the Appendix for more information about room setups).

1. Provide the meeting name and its objectives.
2. Identify how the meeting will be posted in the hotel, if at all.
3. Provide a one-page dossier of all of the contacts, which should include the names, titles, phone numbers, fax numbers, email and cell phone numbers of the following:
   * Facility contacts
   * Your organization's contacts
   * On-site contacts
   * Emergency contacts
   * Ground transportation contacts
   * Air travel contacts
   * Décor
   * Entertainment
   * Speakers
   * A/V
   * Gifts / Amenities
   * Production
   * IT
   * Security

Meeting / Event Information and Effective Dates	
Meeting / Event Name:	
Start Date	
End Date	
Meeting # (if automated through a meeting management technology)	
Contract Signature Date:(date that the contract must be signed by)	
If a request is received by another party for the same arrangements, Hotel shall notify our Organization in writing and our Organization shall have three business days to respond from the time of notification by Hotel in writing to sign and return this Agreement.	

Function Space

All function space must be listed per day in the table below (breakfast room, general session room, breakout room(s), office, lunch room, technology room, storage room, reception room, dinner room, etc.).

Function Space Example:								
Date	Start time	End time	Function	# of people	Setup type	Room name	Sq. footage	Audio-visual
5/1/11	7:00 AM	12:00 AM – 24 hour hold	General Session	100	Classroom	Ballroom A	3,000	12 flip charts with markers 1 screen 1 LCD 2 Lav Mics
Use table below or provide computer generated version with contract:								
Date	Start time	End time	Function	# of people	Setup type	Room name	Sq. footage	
Last day of meeting	7:00 a.m.		Luggage storage					

Room Block

Room Block Information								
	Day 1	Day 2	Day 3	Day 4	Day 5	Day 6	Day 7	
Room Type	[insert date]	[insert date]	[insert date]	[insert date]	[insert date]	[insert date]	[insert date]	**TOTAL**
Singles King or Queen bed (1 bed):								
Double / Double Double-beds (2 beds):								
Staff Single:								
Suites:								
Other:								
[fill in as needed]								
TOTAL ROOMS:								

Additional requirements that may be listed in meeting specifications include:

- Audio-visual
- Ground transportation requirements that the hotel will manage (see below)
- Bellstand
- Business center
- Shipping
- Signage
- Certificates of insurance
- Cleaning
- Confidential document handling
- Convention services department – director / manager contact
- Deliveries, faxes and messages
- Destination management company
- Food and beverage expectations
- Function space expectations
  - ➢ Temperature and lighting requirements
  - ➢ Linens
  - ➢ Instructions for cleaning crew
  - ➢ Permanently locked rooms instructions and key information
  - ➢ Airwall expectations

- Green initiatives
- Post-convention report expectations
- Radio communications expectations
- Crisis management plan expectations

Food and Beverage

Food and beverage is one of the most important aspects of your meeting. People either love it or complain about it. Never underestimate the importance of attendee satisfaction when it comes to food and beverage options. It will also be the second or third largest spend category. Typically, sleeping rooms and air travel are the leading two cost factors of meetings, with food and beverage being the third biggest expense. Of course, every meeting is different.

Food and beverage is one of the places where a budget can escalate quickly. Think about what will be offered for:

> - Will catered meals / breaks be included in our meeting? Which meals / breaks? Will we use sit-down service or buffets? Do we need box lunches for the day of departure? Will we have a reception before dinner?
> - Will alcohol be served?
> - Will any meals be taking place off-property (at a place other than the meeting venue?)
> - Is there a minimum amount of money we need to spend on food and beverage?

- Breakfast (continental, buffet, or plated with regular and decaf coffee, tea, fruit juices, soft drinks and water)
- A.M. Break (replenish drinks)
- Lunch (buffet or plated) (Some meeting planners eliminate dessert from the lunch menu and then provide both healthy snacks and sweet treats at the PM break.)
- P.M. Break (replenish drinks, snacks)
- Reception (pre-dinner) (determine if alcohol will be served with hors d'oeuvres)
- Dinner (buffets, themed food stations, plated)

Professional meeting planners usually work with the chef to create unique menus. Without that specialized skill, work with your Convention Services Manager who will be able to help you create a menu.

Consider where the food and beverage will be served. While it is possible to have the food and beverage in the same room as the meeting room, it is not usually recommended because attendees like to have a different environment than the meeting room they occupied all morning. Often times breakfast, breaks, and lunches are held outside of the meeting room or in a separate room.

Note that if you opt to have food services set inside your meeting room, you may be disrupted by hotel staff setting up in the middle of your meeting.

Alternatively, serving food inside the meeting room may be necessary if the agenda allows little or no time for meal functions. Some meals are eaten during the meeting itself and termed a "working meal" – where lunches become "working lunches" and dinners "working dinners".

It is important to remember that some people may not show up for meals. For example, if you are planning a multi-day meeting, some people may not show up for your breakfast on the second day. Keep this in mind as you are guaranteeing your attendance numbers with the hotel or venue.

Serving alcohol often challenges meeting planners. For more information on how to manage communications regarding alcohol, see the Appendix.

Whether you have a small meeting or a large event, professional meeting planners know that food allergies, sensitivities, and religious observances, are important considerations. Always ask your attendees if they require special food. In addition, you may want to consider talking to the chef and asking him / her to label food to meet the following food sensitivities / allergies:

- Vegetarian and / or vegan
- Low fat
- Low sodium
- Low cholesterol
- Low carbs
- Gluten-free
- Shellfish
- Nuts
- High protein
- Dairy
- Beef / pork (etc.)
- Kosher
- Halal

There are numerous food and beverage pricing methods to consider and the best thing to do is to ask your Convention Services Manager for the best method of pricing within your budget. For example, prices may be per gallon (coffee, tea, hot water), per person, per appetizer, per family style meal or per entrée. Even the drinks may be priced using various methods such as per drink, per person per hour, or per bottle. Whenever possible, ask for pricing on drinks to be on consumption so that bottles that are unopened can be returned to the hotel or venue.

In addition to using your hotel property or caterer to plan your food and beverage needs, there is another option that is gaining popularity with many corporations that seek ways to enhance the meeting attendees' culinary experience and save money at the same time. Many restaurants are ideal for small to mid-size meetings of 5 people to 100 or more attendees. Frankly, restaurants are usually an easy, wise choice for meeting planners because of the quality of food, familiarity of brand, and the comfort of private dining rooms. Combining the restaurant experience with savings, Dinova (www.dinova.net) is a unique service that saves corporations money and increases a greater share of meeting and corporate dining spend with select restaurants. After a corporation signs up with Dinova (at no cost), the savings are automatic when a Dinova network restaurant is used and paid for by a corporate credit card. The card can be a corporate credit card, procurement card, meeting card, or ghost card. There is no "ID card," coupons, or membership numbers involved. The corporation can receive a rebate back to the card used for payment.

See more information on food and beverage in Appendix.

Transportation

Air

Air transportation should be arranged through the organization's preferred travel management company using either an online booking tool designed for groups or through agent-assisted telephone calls. It is not recommended that air travel be booked through a third-party meeting planning company because the organization may lose its opportunity to use pre-negotiated airline rates and its visibility into traveler's whereabouts which could compromise crisis management plans. If air travel is booked through an incentive or meeting planning company other than the preferred travel management company, it is important that the incentive or meeting planning company use the organization's airline contract discounts and that the booked traveler data be available to the organization's travel leaders.

- Is there a limit as to how many of our organization's passengers may be on one plane?
- What travel management company or agency do we use? Can we use the meeting planning company's travel agency or our own agency?
- Do we need ground transportation to pick up attendees from airport? Return them to the airport?

> In one organization, an internal auditor found that four travel management companies were being used: two for transient / business travelers and two for meetings. The internal auditor recommended a more thorough spend and operations analysis. It was uncovered that each of the four travel management companies were charging different prices for tickets and each held numerous airline credits for passengers who were all from the same organization.

Ground

Determine if taxis, shuttle services, limousine, black cars or chauffeured sedans are needed for your attendees.

Meeting planners will usually develop a spreadsheet of the ground transportation transfers that are needed. Unless you have a preferred ground transportation supplier, it is wise to go to bid with at least three suppliers because often, there are differences in fees. Some questions you may want to ask the ground transportation supplier are:

- If you subcontract services, to whom?
- How much is your Certificate of Insurance? (often $5M or more)
- What type of fleet do you use?
- What is the average age of your vehicles?

- Have your drivers been through background checks?
- Do you track your drivers' safety records? What happens to those drivers with violations?
- Who do we contact with changes? Is there a 24/7 dispatcher? How many minutes will it take to make a change?
- Are there wait-time fees?
- Are there no-show / cancel fees?
- Can buses have signage in the windows with our logo?
- Method of payment? deposits required?

When arranging for ground transportation, it is critical that you obtain air manifests that include airport arrival and departure information for each attendee such as:

- Passenger's first and last name
- Passenger's phone number
- Date and time of arrival
- Airline and flight number
- Arrival Airport
- Originating city
- Pick-up location
- Drop off location

Although it may be difficult to review each and every traveler's records for accuracy, you may want to at least do a basic review of the manifest.

Conduct a more *general* review of the manifest to determine trends. You should look for things like arrival and departure patterns to determine peak times and alert vendors accordingly.

Ask yourself the following questions: Are attendees arriving late in morning and missing breakfast thus affecting your meal counts? Are they departing very shortly after the meeting adjourns and skipping lunch or breaks also affecting your meal guarantees? Are attendees arriving a number of days prior to the event? Are they departing a number of days after? If this is the case you may want to revisit your hotel room block.

Perhaps your attendees do not need air at all and will drive in. This too will affect your room block.

Does the budget allow for you to pay for parking for those that are local and driving in?

It is also advised that you conduct a more *specific* review of the manifest. Are there duplicate air bookings? Are there names on the manifest that you do not recognize or who were not invited? When and how are your VIPs arriving? Are your speakers arriving with enough time to prepare for the engagement?

Once the manifest has been adequately reviewed, it will need to be sent to the contracted transportation company (if applicable) so that transfers can be booked accordingly. In return your transportation company should provide you with a list of transportation confirmations that you will need to vet against your manifest.

Be prepared to manage significant additions and changes to your manifest especially in the days leading up to the meeting. Be abreast of these changes and remain in constant contact with your transportation company to react accordingly.

Audio-Visual

Audio-Visual (A / V)

Basic A / V requirements can be supplied by either the hotel's A / V supplier or another preferred supplier. During your hotel contract negotiations, it is important to confirm with the property that you can bring in your own A / V supplier if it is important to you.

Some organizations choose to bring in their own LCD unit from their office. Although it may save your budget, you run the risk of a poor presentation. Your equipment may not be suitable for the meeting room. Additionally, if you experience any technical difficulties, you will not have technical support as you would have if you had rented the equipment from the hotel or from another AV supplier. You may not want to risk an unprofessional presentation for the sake of saving a few dollars.

> - Should we use the hotel's audio-visual supplier? Or, should we use a different audio-visual supplier?
> - If we use our own preferred audio-visual supplier, will the hotel allow it? For what fee?
> - Should we load the presentations on to our own laptops? Should we rent laptops?
> - Should we load presentations from one server? Or individually, machine by machine?

Some basic A / V needs may include the following:

- **Audio (Sound)**
  - Microphones (wireless vs. wired, hand held vs. lavaliere, mics on stands, table top mics)
  - CD player
  - MP3
  - Sound system / speakers

- **Visual (Projection)**
  - LCD Projector (standard or high definition)
  - VCR (via TV monitor or via projection)
  - DVD (via TV monitor or via projection)
  - Monitors (PC, flat screen, plasma)
  - Screen (dual screen, rear screen)
  - Video Camera / IMAG (for interviews, archives, image magnification, satellite broadcast / webcasts)

- **Miscellaneous A / V Needs**
  - Flipcharts
  - White board

- Power strips / extension chords
- Laser pointer
- Wireless mouse
- ARS (Audience Response System – "Polling")
- Provisional iPads[4]

---

4   *The iPad has captured audiences not only because of its fashionable sophistication, but also because of its practicality. With four generations in our workforce, our fluid environments, and the never-ending pursuit to engage attendees better than our competition, the iPad is engaging all audiences, solving most if not all of these concerns, and is becoming the indispensable tool that your meeting requires. A provisioned iPad (an iPad that includes pre-loaded materials with a uniform interface) provides the equipment and solution for effective and powerful content delivery without the risk exposure of Bring Your Own Device (BYOD). If organizations allow BYOD for delivery of meeting content, then data confidentiality, privacy, support, and metrics are unavailable. A company that provides provisioned iPads is SmartSource.

Décor and Entertainment

If you are conducting a formal business meeting you may not be in need of décor or entertainment. However, if you are including a social program or networking opportunities, you may want to consider including décor and entertainment if your budget allows.

With décor and entertainment, you have the flexibility of providing items as simple as balloons and a DJ to more extravagant items like staging, flowers, and headliner entertainers.

The goals and objectives of the meeting will determine the level of décor and entertainment warranted. You will provide different décor and entertainment for a business conference than you would for an incentive event for example. A note of caution--depending on the objective of the meeting, you want to consider how the décor and entertainment will be perceived. If it appears too expensive, attendees may view it as a waste and frivolous. If it appears too cheap, attendees may view it as low quality. It is a challenge to plan the perfect décor and entertainment based on the organization's culture, the people's perception, and a reasonable budget.

There are various options on how to manage décor and entertainment. You can manage these independently or enlist the help of outside resources.

For more simple items like flowers, balloons, DJ – you can manage these items on your own. The hotel concierge can be a great resource for vendor recommendations.

Alternatively, most times your hotel Convention Services Manager can manage these things for you as well but be aware that a service fee may be charged.

For more complex inclusions like lighting, staging, scene sets, headliner entertainers, etc – you may want to work directly with a party planning firm, Destination Management Company (DMC), production company, and enlist the help of a professional meeting planner.

Regardless of how these components are managed, you should negotiate the contracts with as much diligence as you did the hotel contract.

Sometimes you can even barter with vendors and trade your company's services / products for their services / products. You could also offer sponsorship privileges to your vendors. Explore ways to maximize your budget.

Consider piggy-backing on décor items and using the same props for your dinner that another group may have used for their lunch. Perhaps a high-end entertainer is in town for another event. You may considering booking the entertainer while he or she is in town thus saving money on flights and per diem expenses.

Remember some décor can be re-purposed and used at multiple events (ex: flowers at dinner can be used the next day at breakfast).

Finally, be socially responsible and donate leftover décor to others who may appreciate it like flowers to nursing homes, hospitals, shelters, etc.

Gifts / Amenities

Many times a small gift that represents the values of the company or the theme of the meeting will be purchased and placed in sleeping rooms for your attendees. Sometimes only VIPs may receive these items; other times these gifts may be provided to all attendees. There are many options to consider but here are a couple of choices:

- Ask the hotel what types of trays, platters, or amenities they have that could be placed in the room for you. A cheese tray with a small, individual bottle of wine, a tray of chocolates, a basket of fruit or some other combination is always welcomed by weary travelers. Ask the hotel for the different price ranges of these items.

- Find a local gift or incentive company, a gift basket company, a florist, or caterer who would be willing to package baskets, boxes, or bags with goodies such as food, trinkets from the area, bottles of water, books, etc.

Usually you can ask the hotel to print a message on a gift card for you and then place these items in the sleeping rooms. There will most likely be a fee for delivering or "dropping" these items into each room unless you have negotiated this fee as a concession. Speaking of concessions, there are also ways to get a few of the food trays complimentary. Remember to see www.TEPlus.net for more information about contracts and concessions.

Green Initiatives

The Green Meeting Industry Council website lists a six-step process, best practices, and case studies for greening your meetings. Work with your venue and suppliers to optimize your greening efforts. For the purpose of this Playbook, we list a few ideas below for you to consider:

- Instead of sending hard copy brochures, registration cards, invitations, or printed hand-outs / materials onsite, please consider using online alternatives.

- Use recycled paper and products

- Encourage shuttles, carpools and public transportation use

- Purchase "living arrangements" or whole fruit centerpieces that can be reused or work with the hotel to donate the fruit to a local non-profit

- Sparingly place paper and pens in the middle of the table for the few people who may need it, rather than placing them at every seat

- Remind attendees to turn off lights and air-conditioning when not in their rooms

- Contract with a hotel that offers reuse of linens and towels

- Collect unused soap and toiletries for local shelter donations

- Support local – (farmers, suppliers, etc.)

- Request bulk – (water containers, sugar, cream, etc., rather than individual bottles or packages)

- Encourage attendees to use the proper receptacles (paper, glass, plastic, aluminum)

- Reduce or eliminate disposable items such as paper napkins, plastic serving ware

Rooming List

You have 2 options when it comes to making sleeping room reservations:

1. Attendees contact the hotel directly to book their own reservations.
2. Room requests are collected and compiled. A "rooming list" must then be created and submitted to the hotel to book the rooms.

This option you choose is largely based on the desired method of billing.

One booking option is for your *attendees to contact the hotel* and book their own reservations. This method should only be used when guests are paying for their own sleeping rooms. Charges can be posted to personal credit cards or to corporate cards. The attendee can then absorb the cost themselves or be reimbursed via their expense reports. Although this method requires less work on the part of the meeting organizer, it also affords less control over your attendee's reservations and thus your contracted room block.

The second option is to collect room requests and submit a report or *"rooming list"* to the hotel. This task may be done using a technology system or manually. If sleeping rooms are to be paid for directly by the company, this is the best method of booking rooms. As these rooms are fully paid for by the organization, you will want full control over these costs. Additionally, you can have full control over room assignments, dates you will host charges, room upgrades, discounted rates, etc.

The "rooming list" method of booking sleeping room reservations can also be used if the attendee is paying for their own charges. Since you will not be collecting credit card information (risky due to identify exposure), your organization will be expected to guarantee the reservations to your hotel master account. Guests will present their credit cards at hotel check in and at that time, the organization will be released of their obligation. Should a guest no-show, the organization will incur the no-show fee and it will be posted to the master account.

Rooming lists should be compiled with bookings listed alphabetically by last name. This can be downloaded from the meeting management technology into Excel. Collect data such as check in date, check out date, room type, billing, "share with" assignments if sharing rooms are required, VIPs, special needs, etc. Below is a screenshot sample of a typical rooming list.

Last Name	First Name	Participant Type	Room Type	Check-In	Check-Out	Requested Shoulder Dates	No Of Nights	Special Requirements	Hotel Billing Instructions	Notes
Doe	Jane	Host	Suite Upgrade	1-May	3-May		2	VIP	MBA	
Losurdo	Susan	Meeting Planner	King - Staff Rate	1-May	3-May		2		MBA	NEW ADD
Scholar	Debi	Speaker	King	1-May	4-May	5/3/2013	3	non-smoking room	MBA, IPO for shoulder dates	
Smith	John	Staff	King	29-Apr	3-May	4/29/13, 4/30/13	4		MBA, IPO for shoulder dates	
Tiley	Joe	General	King	2-May	3-May		1		MBRT	DATE CHANGE

Changes:
highlighted in yellow
specific change bolded in red

Billing Key:
MBA = Master Bill All charges
MBRT = Master Bill Room & Tax only
IPO = Individual Pays Own charges

Regardless of your booking method, the hotel should provide you with a report of your groups "sleeping room confirmations". You may request these reports as often as needed. These confirmations must be reviewed (if individuals called in) and vetted (if a rooming list was submitted).

Another report that the hotel should supply is called a "room block pick up report". This is a report of how many rooms you have booked on each night. This is especially helpful when comparing the booked rooms against the contracted block. Monitor this report closely to ensure contracted obligations are being met. If obligations are not met, the corporation will incur penalties (called "attrition"). If the block is monitored early and often, the organization may have the opportunity to reduce their contracted room block. Extra rooms may be released back into general hotel inventory so that the hotel can attempt to resell them to the public. The organization will not be responsible for any rooms resold.

Room reservation additions, changes, and cancellations happen often. If you are operating with a rooming list, be prepared to submit these changes in writing as soon as the changes become known. It is recommended that changes be included in the master rooming list. Make sure to highlight any changes in a different color for the hotels ease. Remember to request the confirmation report from the hotel after each round of change submissions.

Paying for sleeping rooms is usually done using one of the three following methods:

- Master Bill Room and Tax Only (MBRT)
- Master Bill all Charges (MBA)
- Individual Pays Own Charges (IPO)

Meeting / event charges for MBRT, MBA, or the charges that the Individual does not pay, should be paid on a Meetings Card or Procurement Card so that total meeting expenses can be reconciled and reported.

Meeting charges should not be placed on a Corporate Card unless absolutely necessary for a couple of reasons:

- It is more challenging to track meeting spend on a corporate card
- The cardholder may accrue membership rewards points on meeting spend, which is not appropriate

Only if a supplier will not accept the Meeting Card or Procurement Card, then charges may be invoiced and paid through Accounts Payable.

Confirming Logistics and Banquet Event Orders

After you supply the hotel with your meeting specifications, rooming lists, reports, etc. – the hotel will in turn provide documentation that confirms their understanding of your needs. This documentation will require your review, approval, and sometimes your signature.

The hotel will provide you with *Banquet Event Orders (BEO's)* confirming all of your meeting room and catering arrangements. These documents are extremely important because most hotels will consider this information as the "updated contract" and will hold you liable for the costs of everything that is documented in the BEO. Review your BEO very carefully. Be sure to review:

- Meeting/event name and dates
- Start and end times
- Number of people
- Room names
- Authorized signors
- Room setup requirements
- A/V
- Food and beverages
- Other special requests / requirements

Submit your food and beverage guarantees

Your BEO's will note the number of people attending. You will be required to confirm your final headcount as the meeting nears. This is otherwise known as submitting your *"guarantees"*. This typically happens 72 hours prior to your event. See your hotel contract for specific date requirements. Once your headcount is "guaranteed" – you may not decrease headcount or increase headcount significantly. You will be financially responsible for what you guaranteed regardless of actual attendance. For this reason it is important to consider factors that may affect attendance (for example: meal times, arrivals / departures, no-shows, etc).

Also be aware of the hotels "overset policy". This policy outlines a percentage (typically 3-5%) to which the hotel will prepare and overset food. For example, if your hotels overset policy is 5% and your headcount is 100 people, the hotel will prepare food and service for 105 people. You are not charged for these extra 5 meals unless they are consumed.

Review and sign Audio-Visual orders

Oftentimes AV companies reside onsite at the hotel/venue but operate independently. They may require you to sign AV orders that act as secondary contracts (similar to BEO's). Review these orders carefully before signing. Many times, minor changes will happen on-site so prepare for this reality and budget accordingly.

Compare Rooming Lists to Manifests

Obtain the report of sleeping room confirmations and review/vet:

- Accurate spelling of names
- Correct arrival and departure dates
- Room types
- Share with assignments (if applicable)
- VIPs
- Billing
- Special needs

Review and sign other vendors' orders

Other vendors may have similar documents for review, signature, and headcount guarantee (for example: restaurants, décor, entertainment, gifts, printed materials, etc.).

Obtain transportation confirmation reports and review them for accuracy. Confirmations should be vetted against the manifests and group transportation requests you supplied.

Compare your rooming list against your travel manifests to uncover discrepancies in arrival / departure dates vs. check in/check out dates.

Billing Arrangements

You will need to submit a Direct Bill Application to the hotel. A company needs to be approved for direct billing before a master account can be set up. If your company does not have adequate credit, then the venue will require a significant deposit or even full prepayment. Direct Bill Applications can take up to 30 days to be processed so this should be addressed during the contract stage. A best practice is to use a Meeting Card or Procurement Card to pay for your meeting /event instead of a check.

Invoice Expectations

You may want to request that your invoices are itemized. For example, you could require that the hotel invoice be itemized into:

- Will attendees pay their own hotel bill and incidentals? Or, will it the room and tax be master billed with incidentals going to their corporate card? Or, everything master billed so the attendees do not have to pay anything directly?

- Sleeping rooms / tax (also itemize for no-shows, attrition)

- Food and beverages (also itemize bartender fees / alcohol separate from food)

- Meeting room rental (if applicable)

- Audio-visual

- Telecommunications

- Transportation and miscellaneous (guest room Internet, business center, power, etc.)

You will need to determine the charges that will be master billed vs. individually charged. For example, you could explain to the hotel that the following charges will be billed to the Organization's master account:

- Sleeping rooms and tax charges (must include folios)

- Group meals / beverages (must include signed banquet checks)

- Meeting room rental, business center, engineering, telecommunications charges (must include signed documentation approving charges)

- Hotel parking

- Audio-visual equipment and office rental fees (must include signed A / V checks)

- All applicable taxes and gratuities

You may want to notify the hotel that individuals are responsible for sleeping room incidental charges at check out.

Give the hotel the name and contact information for the person in your organization that will ultimately review the final invoice and authorize it for payment. Most likely, this person will be you.

For all suppliers (e.g. audio-visual, ground transportation, décor, etc.) always ask for an itemization of costs, not one lump sum.

Be prepared to review and pay multiple invoices given the number of suppliers that provided services or product for the meeting / event.

Crisis Management

All meetings should have a Plan B and a Plan C in case Plan A is diverted due to some form of a crisis. Crises may include natural hazards (e.g. weather related, black-outs) or human-caused events, accidental and intentional, (e.g. suicides, transportation accident, terrorist attacks).

There is more information in how to prepare for meeting crises in Scholar and Losurdo's **"Crisis Management Handbook: A Quick Reference Guide for Meeting Planners"** available on Amazon and iTunes.

> • What will we do if there is a crisis during our meeting?
> • Do we have a Crisis Management Team in our organization? Do we have all of their contact information?
> • Who do we call? What do we do?

The primary activities to consider for meetings that may encounter a crisis are:

- Getting the professionals involved as soon as possible (e.g. calling 911, or others as applicable)
- Accounting for all of the attendees through some form of a check-in process
- Securing hotel space, ground transportation, or evacuation services for attendees to either stay in the area or leave as necessary
- Identify the right path for escalation of information (e.g. organization's security team, human resources, etc.)
- Journaling all information for incident reporting as applicable

See Appendix H for Important Numbers and Data that will be useful in times of a crisis.

> During a crisis situation at one organization, all meetings were required to be registered in one technology system. When the Crisis Assessment Team joined a conference call to identify which attendees needed to be evacuated from the region, one of the people on the conference call stated that "we missed a group that needs to be evacuated." Puzzled, the team once again reviewed the meeting management technology for all of the meetings registered and did not see this particular meeting taking place in the region.
>
> The team quickly realized that the one meeting, and its attendees, had not been registered in the meetings management technology and, as a result, was not on the list for evacuation consideration.
>
> When meetings are held locally, attendees do not fly to a meeting; yet, the meeting should still be registered in a meetings management technology system for the purposes of tracking, budgeting, planning, and crisis management.

Onsite at the Meeting

1. Pre-Convention Meeting ("Pre-Con")

Prior to your arrival, you should schedule a time to meet upon your arrival with hotel department heads and other vendors that will be supporting your event. This is the ideal time to meet your experts personally, as you will be working closely with them throughout the meeting. This may also be a good time to introduce these experts to other key players involved with the meeting. At this meeting, expectations can be set, last minute changes can be made, important deliverables communicated, and questions answered. It is most efficient when you meet with all of the players to discuss high-level deliverables. After these have been discussed, key departments may stay behind to delve further into detail (e.g., convention services, banquets, chef, A / V, etc.). Typically, banquet contracts are re-reviewed for accuracy and last-minute changes. Consider meeting with the following Hotel contacts when the program warrants: General Manager, Sales, Catering / Convention Services, Reservations, Front Desk, Housekeeping, PBX, Room Service, Restaurant, Chef, Banquets, Convention Setup, Transportation / Parking, Engineering / Electrical, Business Center, Shipping & Receiving, Health Club / Spa, Security, Accounting, etc. Outside Vendors: A / V / Telecom, Production Company, DMC, Transportation, Decor / Entertainment, On-site temp staff, Outside Security, etc.

2. Office and Registration Setup

Upon arrival at your meeting location, one of your first priorities is to setup your office and / or registration space. This is your command center (or control room) for all operations and attendee contact.

- Posting: Clearly post your office / registration locations with appropriate signage. Include hours of operation.

- Office / Registration Equipment: Your office / registration needs may vary with the program's complexity and level of attendees. Complex offices could require office equipment (e.g.,: printers, fax, copier, shredders, phones, Internet connections, power, walkie-talkie radios, etc.). This equipment needs to be inventoried and tested and instructions clearly posted.

- "Lock-out": It is recommended that you request to have these spaces on "lock-out" meaning that this space is accessible only to those you grant keys to, and hotel security. You will want to inventory these keys, distribute them, and make sure to collect them at event's end.

- Break Stations: You may want to provide beverages and light snacks to your on-site support staff working in your office / registration.

3. Locate and Inventory Your Incoming Shipments

Upon arrival, it is critical to meet with the in-house Shipping & Receiving (S&R) Department to locate all of your in-coming shipments. Make sure to come with all the tracking information so that stray packages can be tracked and located. Once your packages are located you may request to have the S&R Department deliver the boxes to your office, registration, guest room, meeting room, etc. Note that depending on the number and weight of your boxes, S&R fees may apply. Once the boxes are delivered to their end location, open and inventory the contents of each box to make sure you are not missing any items. Set up your supplies / goods as necessary.

4. Conduct a Briefing With On-Site Support Team

If you have an internal team of staff that will provide on-site administrative support (administrative assistant, registration, room setup, etc.), you will want to conduct a briefing with them as a group. Here you can discuss the objectives of the event, event schedule, hot buttons, duties, problem escalation, etc. You can also set expectations for hours of work, dress code, behavior, service levels, etc. It is also advisable that you give a tour of the hotel space so that you and the team know where rooms and services are located.

5. Assemble Registration / Meeting Materials

Usually your registration / meeting materials are not assembled prior to arrival. Prior to attendees arriving and the registration / meeting start, you may need to gather your staff to assemble these materials. Such materials may include name badges / lanyards, packets, agendas, personalized confirmation sheets, speaker bios, maps, promotional inserts, bags, pads, pens, portfolios, vouchers, gifts, etc. Once registration materials are assembled, they should be filed alphabetically behind the registration desk for ease of distribution. Other materials that need to be set on tables inside meeting rooms will need to be organized by day / time / meeting room for ease of setup.

6. Monitor Arrivals and Departures

You may or may not be providing hosted transportation services to and from local airports, train stations, offices etc.

- If you are providing transportation, you will have collected travel itineraries from your attendees. These itineraries will help your transportation company to arrange the transfers and help you to monitor arrivals and departures, especially during peak times. Transportation companies can also help you to track flights and locate passengers, etc. This itinerary information will also prove useful to the hotel as well as your internal on-site support staff, as it will help to arrange staff for front desk, housekeeping, and conference registration / office accordingly.

- If you are not providing transportation, you may or may not have collected travel itineraries in advance. If you collected travel itineraries, see above. If you have not collected travel itineraries you can estimate peak arrivals and departures based on hotel check-in / check-out patterns, past history, event agenda, etc. You may want to share your estimates with hotel front desk, hotel drive-up (to prepare for taxi / shuttle demand), and internal on-site support.

7. Bill Reviews

- Conduct daily bill reviews and identify any charges in question. Discrepancies addressed on-site are far more likely to get resolved. Note that in order for your venue to collect all of the bills and perform necessary audits, you will most likely receive invoices the day following the events (e.g., you will be presented with Monday's bills on Tuesday morning). If possible, conduct a final bill review on the final day of the program to ensure all charges are correct and all adjustments have been made.

- Confirm when the final bill will be sent to you; request a paper copy as well as an electronic copy and back-up documentation).

8. Tips and Thank-You notes

- Tipping[5] is discretionary, not automatic. The hotel staff is being paid to do their jobs and tipping should be done when individuals go above and beyond their normal duties. Please receive approval from your meeting requester or meeting budget holder before tipping.

- A nice thank-you note or card should go along with your tip.

- **Tip:** Voluntary amount given for good service at an individual's discretion

- **Gratuity:** Mandatory and automatic amount added to bill for service personnel, who receive the entire amount

- **Service Charge:** Mandatory and automatic amount added to bill for service personnel and the facility, each receiving a portion

Customary Tips

Tips may differ based on your location, the total meeting spend, and the type of property you are using. The best thing to do is to ask local meeting planners for their recommendations on the tip amounts.

Staff Member Role	Suggested Tip (Range)	Comments
Banquet Captain or Maitre d'	$50 - $200	Based on number of functions and complexity (a gratuity may not be extended for a buffet dinner, but would be for a plated meal and food stations where there is more work involved).
Chef(s)	$75 - $100	Based on how involved they were (menu customizations, negotiated pricing, did more with less, checked the buffets themselves, corrected any issues, etc.).
Conference Concierge (Red coat)	$25-$50 per day	This fee is for however many days they were actually on duty and helping the group.
Convention Services Manager (CSM)	$200-$500	Based on complexity and level of service they provided.
Doorman and Valet	$2 - $5 per car	Clarify if this is being covered by the Firm.

---

5   Numerous references were obtained including The Essential Guide for Meeting and Convention Planners and the Palm Beach County Convention and Visitors Bureau

Staff Member Role	Suggested Tip (Range)	Comments
Drivers (bus, town car)	N / A	Clarify if tips are being covered in the price of the transfers; then tip would not be applicable. Usually this is the case.
Guest Room Reservation Coordinator	$50 - $100	Based on the size of the group, different room types and number of special requests, etc.
Hotel Bellmen	$2 - $5 per item	Clarify if tips for personal luggage will be covered by the firm or individual. If covered by the individual, then the on-site team should tip for box moves, delivery of items, etc. Tip cards should be used in this instance.
Hotel Housekeepers	$5 per housekeeper per day	Clarify if the Organization is covering tips or if attendees will tip on their own. Confirm with the hotel how many housekeepers are servicing the groups' rooms, and tip per housekeeper. ($5 per day; 20 maids x $5 x 3 nights = $300). Most hotels suggest a charge per room per night. (100 rooms per night, $2 per room, x 3 nights = $600
Housemen	$25 - $75 per person	Based on the number of turns, re-sets, complexity of room setups.
Tour Guides	N / A	Clarify with DMC that tips are being covered in the price of the activity, which is standard. Make sure that the DMC advises the guides that this is how it's being handled.

Optional Tips

Staff Member Role	Suggested Tip (Range)	Comments
Accounting Coordinator	$50 - $100	Optional (very rare and would only be done for a highly complex bill that was presented in a perfect format, with all of the back-up attached).
A / V, IT or Technology (Phones) Staff	$50 - $150	Optional (based on the complexity of the program).
Convention Services Assistant	$50 - $100	Optional (not common to tip, would be done if this person stepped in for the CSM and really contributed to the success of the program, as opposed to just doing the BEOs).
Destination Mgmt Company (DMC)	N / A	A letter to their supervisor is appropriate.
Front Desk Manager or Individual Staff	$50 - $100	Optional (based on size of group, number of changes, challenging customers at the front desk, etc.).
Golf Pro or Tournament Manager	$75 - $100	Optional (based on size and nature of tournament).

Staff Member Role	Suggested Tip (Range)	Comments
Golf Tournament (other staff)	Varies	Optional tips may be considered for other staff members who assist with a tournament again based on size and nature of the tournament. For example, for a large tournament with lots of bag handling you may consider a $5-$10 per bag tip for those who load / unload clubs.
Ground Transportation Coordinator (overall)	$50 - $100	Optional (based on the size of the program, number of transfers, changes, off-site events, etc.).
Hotel Concierge	$25	Optional and not commonly tipped; if they have assisted with Dine Around or any special arrangements.
Off-site Caterer	N / A	Optional and not commonly tipped.
Shipping and Receiving Staff	$50 - $100	Optional (based on number of boxes shipped, number of moves, etc.). Often one staff member services the PwC on-site office.
Spa Coordinator	$75 - $100	Optional (based on size of program, number of changes, interaction with attendees and ability to get them into their preferred appointments, etc.). Note: this is separate from the massage staff, as their standard gratuity of 15-25% is added to charges automatically for groups.
Transportation Coordinators (loads buses, etc.)	$25 - $100	Optional and not commonly tipped (depends on size and scope of meeting; if someone goes above and beyond, a tip may be warranted).

Notes

A Typical Day

Understand a typical day in the life of an on-site meeting planner.

- A meeting planner's day starts early and ends late. It is not uncommon for her or him to be checking on rooms, food and beverage service and A / V as early as 6:00 a.m. and working as late as 11:00 p.m. You will be the first person to arrive each day and the last person to leave. For example, if breakfast starts at 7:00 a.m. you may be arriving to check rooms and buffets as early as 6:00 a.m. If your dinner / evening event closes at midnight, you will be there to close the event, escort attendees out, tear out and verify the beverage consumption, etc. Unless there are many meeting planners assigned to the meeting, expect to work many hours on-site.

- Always wear comfortable shoes within dress code.

- Be prepared to be accessible 24 hours a day via cell and / or walkie-talkie radio.

- Problems may happen on-site but it is up to the meeting planner to keep this invisible to the attendee.

- Work closely with your hotel, vendors, and on-site support teams to provide direction and support.

- Address attendee issues as they arise.

- Open and close Meeting Registration and On-Site Office according to schedule.

- Unlock meeting rooms as necessary.

- Check the meeting room (setup, test A/V / IT / Electrical equipment, room temperature, registration desk, signage, food service, handouts, badges, sign-in sheets, etc.)

- Check in with speakers / instructors. As you are checking meeting room setups you may have the opportunity to assist your speakers / instructors with last-minute needs. They could need your assistance with minor setup changes, testing a presentation, making copies, or just wanting general information.

- Review your signage, easels, and postings of the directions, meeting rooms, etc. Additionally, hotels and event facilities typically post events internally as well as in their common spaces. They may also have electronic "reader boards" that outline all of the events taking place in their facility that day. These "reader boards" may run on lobby monitors or on guest televisions etc. Check these hotel postings for accuracy in times, locations, names, etc. There may be private events that you do not want posted.

- Check the buffets regularly. You will want to work with the banquet captains to continually monitor the buffets and food services. Prior to opening doors and serving, walk through the buffets to make sure they are set up for ease of flow and that all contracted food items are set and labeled. Instruct banquet staff to replenish or close buffets only with your approval. If your meeting is scheduled to start in 15 minutes, you may instruct banquets to begin clearing and chime attendees into session. You may choose to keep buffets open later to allow for your internal on-site support staff to eat. You may also request to have certain buffet items brought to your break stations or office. As a conscious practice, you may request to have leftover foodstuffs donated to a local shelter. Finally, you may want to consult with the banquet captains to see which items were most and least popular so that you can adjust your menus / quantities for subsequent days.

- Refresh and reset rooms during break / meal times.
- Position staff in public areas during times of meeting transition to direct attendees to next sessions / events.
- Protect confidentiality of all materials; determine if the materials can be disposed of through the hotel's process or if shredders / shred bins are required.
- Secure meeting rooms when not in session and especially at night's end.
- Request daily "MOD" reports from hotel. Manager On Duty (MOD) reports are a record of any issues that may have happened to a hotel guest overnight. Upon request a hotel can provide you this information if it is about an attendee of your conference. If an attendee is injured or is ill or files a complaint, this is information you will want to know so that you may address this and follow up with the guest / hotel accordingly. If there were any security issues, these will also need to be addressed and potentially escalated / reported.
- Request daily in-house, no-show, and hotel occupancy reports. This will help you to monitor attrition if applicable. Additionally, this will provide useful when trying to locate attendees / speakers, etc.
- Conduct a daily bill review and identify any charges in question (see above).

Invoice Reconciliation

1. Review the invoices
2. Confirm that all invoices and the back-up documentation have been received.
3. Comparison Checklist:
   - Compare the final Banquet Event Order (BEO) to any changes noted on the final invoice provided by the hotel. Review the attendee and food / beverage guarantees submitted to the hotel. Onsite, changes may have occurred and as a result, charges may have been incurred.
   - Per your earlier instructions to the hotel, they should have the charges itemized into the following categories:
     - ➢ Sleeping rooms / tax (also itemize for no-shows, attrition)
     - ➢ Food and beverages (also itemize bartender fees / alcohol separate from food)
     - ➢ Meeting room rental (if applicable)
     - ➢ Audio-visual
     - ➢ Telecommunications
     - ➢ Transportation
     - ➢ Miscellaneous (guest room Internet, business center, power, etc.)
     - ➢ Activities (e.g. Spa, Golf, etc.)
   - Compare hotel sleeping room folios to your rooming list. Ensure that arrival / departure dates are correct, no extended stays or incidentals were added to the master account, the room rates are accurate, and any special circumstances for single / double rooms are accounted for correctly. If you received comp rooms, make sure they are deducted from the master invoice. Compare your actual room pick-up to the daily room block occupancy reports; compare the no-show reports generated during the meeting.
   - Compare the contract clauses to the penalties incurred (attrition, cancellation) to verify any fees incurred.
   - Compare the meeting room rental charges to the contracted meeting room rental to verify charges.
   - Compare technology / communications charges with the contracted rates including discounts negotiated.
   - Compare audio-visual orders, BEO and charges noted to the final bill provided by the hotel with the contracted rates including discounts negotiated.
   - Compare office equipment rentals outlined on the BEO's or contracts to the invoice to verify rates, amount of equipment, and that the dates charged are accurate. Ensure that discounts were applied if negotiated.
   - Review costs of copies, shipping, freight, entertainment, supplies with the contracted rates.
   - Compare ground transportation manifests and charges to contracted rates including discounts that were negotiated.

- Ensure that deposits have been applied, and subtract this amount when processing the last invoice and payment.
- Deduct credits that may have been used from previous meetings or complimentary concessions.

4. Review and confirm that the air transportation costs are accurate.

- Post Air Cost Reports include:
    - Passenger Name
    - Air routing
    - Departure date
    - Date of charge
    - Billing date
    - Debit / Credit Indicator
    - Billing amount (including any service fees if applicable)
    - Charge description
    - Ticket number
    - Air ticket issuer
    - Air class of service
    - Air carrier code

5. Pay for your meeting or event.

6. Debrief and identify improvements for the next meeting or event.

7. Report your success through the use of metrics that may need to be produced.

8. Store your contracts and documents according to your organization's document retention policy.

9. Obtain the actual attendance and cost for each function from the venue.

10. Reconcile and process invoices. Document the estimated budget vs. the actual cost and the difference.

> Because of the multiple hotel departments that charge an invoice (catering, housekeeping, IT, etc.), it is common to find errors on hotel invoices. Be sure to check the invoice carefully and dispute charges that you do not believe are correct. And, it is a good time to remind you that hotel contracts and concessions are an extremely important contributor to your final invoice. Before the contract is signed, it is important to negotiate the cost of items for simple things like moving boxes, electrical cords, flip charts, etc.

Survey

After the meeting concludes, consider sending a survey using the meeting management technology, SurveyMonkey (or similar tool), or via a more manual method such as email. If you have more than 5-10 attendees, it is time consuming to calculate all of the surveys manually. Use an automated tool to help you accomplish this survey goal.

Below are some sample questions you may want to ask your attendees:

Speaker	(Name) duplicate for as many speakers as you have					
Do you agree or disagree that the speaker fulfilled your expectation of the session?	Strongly disagree	Disagree	Neutral	Agree	Strongly Agree	Not Applicable (e.g. did not attend)
Speaker's presentation skills	Very poor	Poor	Average	Good	Excellent	Not Applicable (e.g. did not attend)
What are your suggestions on improvement?	(Comment area)					
Destination and Transportation						
City / Location	Very poor	Poor	Average	Good	Excellent	
Air Transportation Services	Very poor	Poor	Average	Good	Excellent	Not Applicable (e.g. did not need to travel to meeting)
Ground Transportation Services	Very poor	Poor	Average	Good	Excellent	Not Applicable (e.g. did not use)
Comments						
Onsite Meeting Registration						
Check-In	Very poor	Poor	Average	Good	Excellent	Not Applicable (e.g. did not stay at hotel)
Registration Materials	Very poor	Poor	Average	Good	Excellent	Not Applicable (e.g. did not pick up materials)
Comments						
Venue / Hotel						
Check-In	Very poor	Poor	Average	Good	Excellent	Not Applicable (e.g. did not stay at hotel)
Sleeping Rooms	Very poor	Poor	Average	Good	Excellent	Not Applicable
Meeting Rooms	Very poor	Poor	Average	Good	Excellent	Not Applicable

Temperature Comfort overall	Very poor	Poor	Average	Good	Excellent	
Food	Very poor	Poor	Average	Good	Excellent	Not Applicable
Audio-visual	Very poor	Poor	Average	Good	Excellent	Not Applicable
Comments						
Communication before the Meeting						
Information about the meeting, hotel, and reservations	Very poor	Poor	Average	Good	Excellent	
Questions answered	Very poor	Poor	Average	Good	Excellent	Not Applicable (e.g. did not ask any questions)
Comments						
What was the best about the meeting?	(Comment area)					
What was the worst about the meeting?	(Comment area)					

Reporting, Debriefs, and Thank-Yous

Reporting

There are hundreds of metrics that a professional meeting planner may want to capture based on the meeting objectives and the budget holder's expectations. Below is a sample of the metrics that you may want to consider reporting after the meeting concludes. It is not expected that all of the metrics will be used. It is an idea-generating list for consideration to measure the success of your meeting or event.

- Attendee satisfaction using survey
- Meeting sponsor / budget holder satisfaction
- Cycle time of the completion of tasks
- Lead time from the time the meeting was conceived to the date of the meeting
- Meeting spend by category (e.g. air transportation, hotel, food and beverage, etc.)
- Savings negotiated (be sure to include the value of the concessions, if penalty credits were reused, etc.)
- Budget forecasted to actual spend differences
- Cost per person per day
- Number of attendees (that participated, no-shows, late, etc.)
- Number of hours it took to plan the meeting (include in-sourced, outsourced support)
- Return on investment – more information on how to calculate the ROI on meetings can be found at www.TEPlus.net

Debrief Checklist

Use this checklist to plan for an effective project debriefing meeting. Each block below should be considered a separate agenda item for the meeting.

The purpose of this meeting is to:

- Review the process roles and responsibilities involved in the project.
- Suggest improvements to the process for the future.

The Project Debriefing meeting was held on **[enter date]** and attended by:

Name	Role	Phone

Role:
Successes:
Areas of Improvement
"What could we have done better during the _____ phase?" Consider meeting registration, sourcing, planning, on-site activities, website development, reconciliation, payment, reporting, etc.

From the Areas of Improvement column of the chart(s), determine which items should be addressed and acted upon. The format of the chart below may help organize this information:

Action Item	Who?	By when?

- Is there anything else about this project that needs to be discussed?
- Has this conversation / meeting been worthwhile?

Thank-You

Don't forget to send a thank you note to your speakers, support staff, suppliers, and others that may be applicable.

Conclusion

Debi: One of the authors, Susan, is one of the best meeting and event planners in the industry. She works long hours, scrutinizes every detail, and produces flawless events and meetings. She knows how to "never let them see you sweat" and has the patience of a saint. Meeting and event planning is hard work and those people who are professional meeting planners enjoy a very rewarding career. But, meeting and event planning is not for those people who dabble, forget to follow-up, only work 9-5, and dislike changes.

Good luck planning your meeting! If you want help, please contact Susan or Debi.

Appendix A – Sample Budget

This sample budget is also available in Excel format if you contact Debi or Susan. It does not include items like exhibits or complex meeting items because this Playbook is for administrative assistants, coordinators, and new meeting planners. For more advanced budget spreadsheets, please refer to MPI, APEX, or other online resources.

< >

		Sat	Sun	Mon	Tues	Wed	Thurs	Fri			
Meeting Name											
Meeting Dates											
Day		Sat	Sun	Mon	Tues	Wed	Thurs	Fri			
Date		[insert date]	[insert date]	[insert date]	[insert date]	[insert date]	[insert date]	[insert date]	Total		
Guest Rooms		# Rooms	# Rooms	# Rooms	# Rooms	# Rooms	# Rooms	# Rooms	Rooms	Rate	Total
Participant Rooms (single occupancy)									0	$	$ -	One participant per room
Participant Rooms (double occupancy)												Two participants share a room
Staff Rooms									0	$	$ -	Rooms allocated to onsite meeting support staff
VIP Suites & Parlors									0	$	$ -	Upgraded rooms for VIPs, Speakers, etc
Total Guest Rooms		0	0	0	0	0	0	0	0		$ -	*pricing inclusive of taxes/resort fees*
Guest Rooms % of budget											*[auto-calculate]*	*Industry Target % = ?*

Food & Beverage - On Site		#ppl	#ppl	#ppl	#ppl	#ppl	#ppl	#ppl	Total People	Rate	Total	
Breakfast (buffet or continental?)									0	$	$ -	
AM Break (coffee service and snacks or beverage service only?)									0	$	$ -	pricing based on 1 hr service.
Lunch (buffet, plated, or boxed?)									0			
PM Break (coffee service and snacks or beverage service only?)									0	$	$ -	pricing based on 1 hr service
All day beverage service												pricing based on coffee, tea, sodas, water from 8am-5pm
Reception (hors d)									0	$	$ -	pricing based on a 1 hr reception with 3 hors d per person. Food only
Dinner (plated or buffet)												
Reception/Dinner Alcoholic Beverages (beer & wine bar, full bar, or wine service only?)									0	$	$ -	pricing based on 1 hr alcoholic beverage service of mid-grade brands. caveat that unsafe to serve alcohol with no food.
Hospitality (non alcoholic bev only, non alcoholic bev and snacks, alcoholic bev and snacks?)												lounge like room where attendees can come to relax, network, and get light refreshments. Pricing based on service from 8am-5pm (alcohol service only for 3 hrs). caveat that unsafe to serve alcohol with no food.
Pre tax & grat On Site F&B costs									0		$ -	
On Site F&B Tax/Gratuity										0%	$ -	
Total Food & Beverage											$ -	
Food & Beverage % of budget											*[auto-calculate]*	*Industry Target % = ?*

Meeting Costs	Per day	Per day	Per day	Per day	Per day	Per day	Per day	Per day	Total Spend	X Rate	
Audiovisual and/or Production									0.00	$ -	Additional AV/Production Labor and electrical power may be needed for large meetings with complex AV needs (ie: video, satellite broadcasting, extensive lighting/sound, etc.) Not needed at all meetings. See vendor for pricing.
Meeting Room Rental									0.00	$ -	Venues typically will charge meeting room rental. Your rental is dependent on the amount of space required. If your space to attendee ratio is high (you have a lot of space but only a few attendees) your rental could be higher
Offsite Event Fees (lo end - bowling alley, mid range - ESPN Zone, hi end - Disney?)									0.00	$ -	Events that take place at another location other than the main event location. Pricing does not include transportation or food & beverage costs.
Telephone (number of phone lines?)									0.00	$ -	Should you have need for an extensive number of internet lines - you could require additional equipment which would increase this cost.
Technology (number of internet lines, power strips, laptops, etc.)									0.00	$ -	Anything that may be needed for the meeting rooms or in the working office
Office Equipment									0.00	$ -	Not needed at all meetings. It is at the discretion of the host as they may want to protect proprietary information, displays, equipment, etc. Also, should you have a large complex meeting with AV/Production Labor - the AV company may require security to guard their equipment overnight.
Security (number of hours / security guards?)									0.00	$ -	additional gratuities are up to the discretion of the meeting sponsor to acknowledge excellent service
Discretionary Gratuities (will need to estimate this based on a .5% of total mtg cost)									1.00	$ -	
Total Meeting Costs										$8.00	
Meeting Costs % of budget										*[auto-calculate] Industry Target % = ?*	

Ground Transportation Costs	#ppl	#ppl	#ppl	#ppl	#ppl	#ppl	#ppl	#ppl	Total People	X Rate	
Arrival Ground Transportation (shuttle buses, sedans, or taxi?)									0.00	$ -	Usually from airport to meeting venue on arrival
Departure Ground Transportation (shuttle buses, sedans, or taxi?)									0.00	$ -	Usually from meeting venue to airport on departure.
Transportation Staff (number of staff? Number of hrs?)									0.00	$ -	Needed for large group moves and VIP transfers. Recommend 1 transportation staff for every 100 people.
Off-site Event Transportation (round trip shuttle buses)									0.00	$ -	Events that take place at another location other than the main event location.
Total Ground Transportation										$ -	
Ground Transportation % of budget										*[auto-calculate] Industry Target % = ?*	

Airfare Costs		Total Flyers	X Rate	
Airfare			$500.00	$ -
Total Airfare Costs				*[auto-calculate] Industry Target % = ?*

Content Costs				
Speakers, Team Building, etc.			**Total Content Costs**	
Total Content Costs			$ -	*[auto-calculate] Industry Target % = ?*

Printing / Collateral				
Brochures, Name tags, etc.			**Total Content Costs**	
Total Printing Costs			$ -	*[auto-calculate] Industry Target % = ?*

Shipping				
Shipping, etc.			**Total Content Costs**	
Total Shipping Costs			$ -	*[auto-calculate] Industry Target % = ?*

Grand Total				$ -

Appendix B – Meeting Invitation / Registration

Should be sent out 6-8 weeks before meeting (or earlier if applicable)

Professional meeting planners frequently use technology systems that allow attendees to register. Systems such as StarCite, Cvent, Lenos, Arcaneo Metron, or SignUp4 provide end-to-end meeting management functionality. Yet, there are hundreds of online registration tools that simply provide registration-only type services. However, keep in mind that these systems have not been approved by your IT department and you may be putting confidential data into the system. For example, if you ask if someone has special needs, that data may be deemed "Personal Identifiable Information" and your organization could be fined if that data is released publicly. As such, it is extremely important to use an automated system that has been evaluated by your IT department or that has met all of the necessary security standards.

When attendees register using one of these systems, it automates the process for meeting planners, saves significant time, and provides detailed information about attendees especially when a crisis occurs. It is far easier to track attendee whereabouts by extracting data from a technology system then searching for attendee data in an Excel sheet on someone's computer.

Regardless of the medium used to invite attendees and collect registrations below are some ideas for you.

Introduction

- The purpose of this meeting is to…
- The objective of this meeting is…
- This meeting will help attendees …
- The target audience for this meeting is…
- suppliers ... [level of attendee, role of attendee, department, etc.]
- This meeting is presented by …

Date and Times

- **Begin and End Times Only:** The meeting will begin at 8:00 a.m. on June 1, 20XX and conclude at 5:00 p.m. on June 3, 20XX.
- **Multiple Sessions:** Session 1 will begin at 8:00 a.m. on June 1, 20XX and conclude at 5:00 p.m. on June 3, 20XX. Session 2 will begin at 8:00 a.m. on June 8, 20XX and conclude at 5:00 p.m. on June 10, 20XX.
- **Combination:** Registration will begin at 8:00 a.m. on June 1, 20XX in the Ballroom Foyer. A buffet lunch will be available from 12:00 p.m. noon to 1:00 p.m. in the Devine Room. The meeting will begin promptly at 1:00 p.m. in the Ballroom. The meeting concludes on 5:00 p.m. on June 3, 20XX. See agenda below for more detailed information.

Location

- The hotel address is:
- The hotel phone number is:
- The hotel fax number is:
- The hotel website is:

Simple Agenda Sample

Monday, June 1, 20XX Devine Meeting Room Great Hotel	
8:00 a.m. – 12:00 p.m.	Arrivals
12:00 p.m. – 1:00 p.m.	Buffet lunch in ABC Room
1:00 p.m. – 2:30 p.m.	Session 1 topic
2:30 p.m. – 2:45 p.m.	Refreshment Break in Foyer outside of meeting room
2:45 p.m. – 3:30 p.m.	Session 2 topic
3:30 p.m. – 4:45 p.m.	Session 3 topic
4:45 p.m. – 5:30 p.m.	Open for your leisure
5:30 p.m.	Meet in lobby for transportation to XYZ Restaurant or unique venue (e.g. museum, sporting event, etc.)
6:00 p.m. – 7:00 p.m.	Reception in ABC location of XYZ Restaurant or unique venue
7:00 p.m. – 9:00 p.m.	Dinner in DEF location of XYZ Restaurant or unique venue
9:15 p.m.	Gather for transportation back to Great Hotel
Tuesday, June 2, 20XX Devine Meeting Room Great Hotel	
8:00 a.m.- 9:00 a.m.	Breakfast in ABC Room
9:00 a.m. – 10:30 a.m.	Session 1 topic
10:30 a.m. – 10:45 a.m.	Refreshment Break in Foyer outside of meeting room
10:45 a.m. – 12:00 p.m.	Session 2 topic
12:00 p.m.	Official meeting adjourned
12:00 p.m.	Buffet lunch with To Go Boxes for those attendees with early departures
	Transportation to airport

Registration Scenarios

The type of information that you should collect from attendees regardless of how you get it, is:

- First name, last name (may want to ask if this is the preferred name for their name tag)
- Company name
- Title
- Phone number (preferred phone, mobile phone, may want FAX number)
- Email address
- Address (street, city, state/province, zip, country)
- Ask if they have any special physical or dietary needs
- Emergency contact information (name of person to contact, phone number, relationship to you)

1. Using a Registration Form – Please complete and return the attached registration from to (name) no later than 5:00 p.m. EST on (day and date). Forms maybe emailed to (email address). [Note: make the form easy to fill in using Word or Excel, if you are not using a technology system, so that they can type in their answers, save, and send it back to you.] Confirmations will be sent on (day and date). If you must cancel your registration, please send an email immediately to (name and email) or call (name and phone number). [Don't forget to attach the registration form].

2. Using a Registration System – In order to register for this meeting, please click on the link below to be connected to the registration system. The registration will close at 5:00 p.m. EST on (day and date). You will receive a confirmation (immediately or within X hours) that your registration was received. Your confirmation will contain information regarding (agenda, flight arrangements, ground transportation, activity selected, etc.). If you need to make changes to your registration or cancel your registration, (log back into the system using your confirmation number, or contact name, email, and phone number).

Air Travel Arrangements

- Book through Online Booking System - Air travel to the meeting may be booked through our online booking tool linked (here). Other methods of booking travel will not be allowed and will not be reimbursed. The flight information will be used to arrange for ground transportation for you. The charge for your ticket will be (placed on your corporate card and you must expense it, or placed on a central card and expensing it will not be necessary). Flight arrangements must be made in the least expensive manner according to the arrival and departure parameters for the meeting. Extended stay, early arrival, alternate airport, additional stopover, refundable ticket, etc. that result in an additional cost from the least expensive ticket cannot be expensed to the meeting charge code. Your flight must arrive prior to (time, day and date). Your departure flight must not depart prior to (time, day and date). For this meeting, all travelers must use coach class. If you need to make changes to your flight arrangements, please (whatever the process is with your online booking tool).

- Call in number – Air travel to the meeting may be booked through our preferred (travel agency). Other methods of booking travel will not be allowed and will not be reimbursed. The flight information will be used to arrange for ground transportation for you. Please call the agency at (phone number) to make your travel arrangements. The charge for your ticket will be (placed on your corporate card and you must expense it, or placed on a central card and expensing it will not be necessary). Flight arrangements will be made in the least expensive manner according to the arrival and departure parameters for the meeting. This may involve using a designated group preferred carrier. Booking requests made outside of these parameters (e.g. extended stay, early arrival, alternate airport, additional stopover, refundable ticket, etc.) that result in an additional cost from the least expensive ticket cannot be expensed to the meeting charge code. Your flight must arrive prior to (time, day and date). Your departure flight must not depart prior to (time, day and date). For this meeting, all travelers must use coach class. If you need to make changes to your flight arrangements, please call (travel agency) at (phone number).

Ground Transportation Arrangements

Travelers are responsible for arranging ground transportation to and from home / office and the airport. You should use the most cost-effective method, as only reasonable ground transportation costs will be reimbursed.

There will be no reimbursement for the use of [rental cars, taxis, shuttles]. Attached below are the driving directions.

Ground transportation in the destination city for the meeting will be handled by:

(determine what option suits your meeting)

- Scenario #1 – Hotel Shuttle. The hotel shuttle runs every (insert time) and can be met at the (insert location).
- Scenario #2 – Cab. The approximate cost of the cab to the hotel is (insert cost). This expense is reimbursable. Cabs can be found (insert location).
- Scenario #3 – Super Shuttle, a shared-ride van that services other local hotels. Reservations (are not needed or are needed and can be made by…). The cost of the shuttle is (insert cost). This expense is reimburseable. The shuttle can be found (insert location).
- Scenario #4 – Ground Transportation Company – Individuals should make reservations by calling (phone number). Reference (our company and meeting name) in order to be put on the master account. Drivers can be met at (insert location).
- Scenario #5 – Ground Transportation Company – Reservations will be made for you using your flight information submitted to the travel agency. For reservation or changes made on or after (date the last travel manifest will be delivered to the you as the meting planner), individuals must contact the ground transportation company directly at (phone number) and reference (our company and meeting name) in order to be put on the master account. Drivers can be met at (insert location).

Meeting and Event Planning Playbook   *Debi Scholar and Susan Losurdo*

Hotel Details

Please review hotel details (linked here or attached).

Room Sharing

Associates will be sharing a room with another attendee. On your registration form (or the automated registration form), you will be given the opportunity to request a roommate. Your roommate must also request you. Every effort will be made to grant all requests. Roommate changes will not me made onsite. If you do not select a roommate, one will be assigned to you. Speakers, managers, directors and vice presidents will receive their own room.

Activities and Events

During this meeting, attendees will be going off-site for (insert event – dinner, recreation, teambuilding activity).

(For all activities, provide)
- Date and time
- Where to meet
- Transportation details
- Appropriate attire (if applicable)
  - Dining – jacket and tie for men
  - Golf – collared shirts and soft spikes are required
  - Outdoor events – hats and sunscreen recommended
  - Teambuilding – comfortable closed toe shoes (e.g. sneakers), light weight comfortable clothing (short sleeve shirts and shorts or jeans). (note that this information may not work in your environment as different cultures

Technology

All attendees should bring their laptop computers. Be sure to also bring:

- Locking cable for your computer
- Power supply

Administrative information

The charge code for this meeting is XXX.

Attire

Business attire (or business casual) is appropriate for this meeting. It is recommended that you bring a jacket or sweater sothat you are comfortable as meeting room temperatures vary.

Registration

Onsite registration will be held on (day and date) from (time period) in the (location) where the meeting will take place.

Gratuities

No tipping is required for group meal functions. However, you should tip bell staff and housekeepers if they provide service to you. Reasonable tips are reimbursable in accordance with our policy.

Meeting Charges

- Scenario #1 – Master Accounts – Room, tax, and group meals for all days of the meeting will be paid directly by our organization. Room costs for early arrivals, extended stay overs, and incidental costs (e.g. telephone calls, etc.) will be charged to individual's credit cards. Airfare and ground transportation will be paid directly by our organization.
- Scenario #2 – Individual Credit Cards – Individuals are responsible for expensing room and tax, airfare, and ground transportation for this meeting.

Questions about the meeting's content should be sent to (name, email and phone number).

Appendix C – Pre-Arrival Letter or Know Before You Go Letter

Should be sent out 1 week before meeting

Before your attendees arrive, you should equip them with information such as how they will be transported to hotel from airport, their attire, the agenda, and any other special information they may need. Below is a sample Pre-Arrival Letter often called a "Know Before You Go" letter.

Thank you for registering to attend the [XXX Meeting] scheduled for [Date(s)] in [XXX City or Location]. Below please find important information.

Upon Your Arrival – Ground Transportation from the Airport to the Hotel

Transportation from the airport to the hotel has been made on your behalf. Your transportation will be provided by [XXX supplier]. Upon your arrival at the [City, Airline Terminal], please proceed to the [wherever the ground transportation company will pick up the traveler]. A "Meet & Greet" representation from [XXX supplier] will be carrying a sign that includes your name and our organization's logo. Once all of your baggage has been collected, you will be escorted to your prearranged transportation to the [Hotel]. Gratuities will be paid by our organization.

Note that your transportation has been booked based on your flight arrangements. If you have changed your flight arrangements after [date], then please contact the [XXX supplier] directly by calling [name of person at XXX supplier] at [phone number].

If you are unable to locate the [XXX supplier], or if you missed your flight, or your flight has been cancelled, please contact [XXX supplier] at [phone number].

Event Name and Hotel Information

Our hotel information is as follows:

[Meeting / Event Name] by [Organization]

[Hotel name]

[Hotel's complete address with street, state, city, country, and zip code]

[Hotel's phone number]

[Hotel's fax number]

[Hotel's website]

[Hotel's check-in time: XX p.m.; Check-out time: XX a.m.]

If you are driving to the [XXX] Hotel, parking is located [where] and costs [$XX.XX] per day. [or, explain that the parking fees are being paid by the organization].

On-Site Support

Our organization has on-site support and a location for all questions or concerns.

The on-site support person(s) is: [name of person] and her / his cell phone number is [phone] and her / his email is [email address].

The on-site support office is located in [name of meeting room].

The on-site support office phone number is: [phone number].

The on-site support office will be open starting at X:00 a.m. / p.m. beginning on [day and date] and the office hours will be X:00 a.m. to XX:00 p.m.

Mobile Community

Attendees will have the entire meeting program in the palm of their hand using the [name of the app] for your iPhone, Android, Blackberry, and iPad designed by [name of company] to deliver the ultimate mobile event experience.

Downloading Instructions:

- Download the app to your Smartphone or iPad. Your login information is:
- Android instructions…
- Blackberry instructions…

You are able to view an up-to-date agenda, hotel and city map, presentations, speaker information, and use the mobile application as an audience response system.

On-site Registration

Registration is located outside of the main meeting room [name of meeting room] beginning at [time] on [day]. The registration desk will be open from [time to time] on [days].

Please wear your name badge at all times.

Agenda

The agenda is as follows:

[Provide agenda. Or, if you would prefer not to share the whole agenda, at least provide the activities so that they know what to bring, wear, etc.]

Session selections

If you have not yet selected your sessions, please contact [name] at [phone number] or at [email address] as soon as possible with your selection(s).

Materials

Please find a link below to download the materials for this meeting. We make every effort possible to gather all presentations prior to the meeting. In the event that presentation materials are submitted late, they will be included on our website [or sent to you] within [X days] after the meeting. There will be no printed workbook or hard copy presentations provided at the event.

Special Dietary Needs / Allergies / Special Needs

If you have not yet informed us of any special dietary needs, allergies, or special needs you have, please contact [name] at [phone number] or at [email address] as soon as possible. We will make every effort to accommodate you.

Activities

Wednesday Business Meeting: Business Casual attire

We suggest sweaters or a light jacket for air conditioned meeting rooms and cooler evenings.

Wednesday Dinner – XXX Resort

- For men – Resort Casual attire - khakis, shirts
- For women – Resort Casual attire - capri pants, khakis, skirts and dresses

Thursday – Golf Outing or Spa

- **Golf Clinic and 9 Holes -** Golf attire - Bermuda length shorts or slacks, collared shirts for men, soft spike shoes. People who registered for golf have selected whether or not clubs needed to be rented. If you are unsure, contact [your name or the person who is in charge of the golf outing].

- **Spa:** If you have not done so already, please schedule your spa appointments by [date]. Appointments must be made in advance by calling [name] at [phone number] between [times] 7 days a week. You may also email [name] at [email]. In her absence, please ask for the manager on duty. Please identify yourself as a [organization] participant attending the [name of the meeting]. After [date], unreserved treatment times will be released back to the general public. A **24 hour cancellation notice** is required for all appointments. Treatments not cancelled by the Attendee will be considered a personal expense. All treatment descriptions may be found on their website: [list website]. You should plan to arrive at your spa appointment at least 30 minutes prior to your appointment time.

Friday – Baseball Game

- **Yankees vs. Red Sox** – casual attire, jeans, shorts, t-shirts, sneakers

There will be great photo opportunities so feel free to bring your cameras. It is also recommended that you bring sunglasses and sunscreen.

Tipping

Gratuities have been provided and paid for by our organization for the bellman, valet, housekeeping and pool attendants. Tip for valet service or non-group services are at your discretion to reward an individual for superior service.

No Show Policy

Please remember that a no-show policy has been implemented for activities at this year's meetings. In general, the no-show charge will apply if you cancel an activity after the Thursday meeting registration and your spot remains unfilled, or if you simply don't show for a Firm-sponsored appointment or activity. You can find details in the meeting website.

Departures - Ground Transportation to Airport

Departure notices from [XXX Supplier] will be given to you [at the meeting or however you plan to hand them out] with your departure flight information and your ground transportation pick-up from the hotel back to the airport. If there are any changes, please notify [XXX Supplier] immediately at [phone number] or [email address].

On behalf of the entire staff of our organization, thank you again for registering to attend the [name of meeting] and we look forward to seeing you in [city]. Should you have any questions or need further information, please contact us.

Regards,

[signature of meeting sponsor]

Appendix D – Sample Room Attrition, Due Dates, and Cancellation Grids

Debi has created an addendum with key terms and concessions that you will want to include in your hotel contract. Contact Debi for a copy of the addendum. Although we have included these sample room, food and beverage attrition and cancellation grids, the contract information can be found online at Debi's blog. We added the attrition and cancellation grids because this information is so important to calculate for your hotel contracts. Ask a hotel to clearly define how much you will owe on the exact date should your attendance fall short of the commitment or if you cancel your meeting. Remember, these terms are negotiable. For more information on hotel contracts, visit www.TEPlus.net.

Our organization may exercise the right to take up to the allowable attrition by the Attrition Due Date with no penalty or guarantee the room block. This shall be calculated on a cumulative basis and based on the final room block.

Room Rates, Room Attrition and Rooming List / Reservation Due Date	
Single-bedded (1 bed):	$XXX.00
Double-bedded (2 beds):	$XXX.00
Staff Single:	$XXX.00
Suites:	$XXX.00
Other:	
[fill in as needed]	
Other	
Applicable Occupancy Tax:	%
Resort Fee (if applicable):	$
Other Fee / Tax:	
Other Fee / Tax:	
Allowable Attrition Percentage	20%
Attrition Due Date:	[insert actual date]
Will be fourteen (14) days prior to the contracted arrival night. On or before this date, our Organization has the right to exercise the cumulative contracted Allowable Attrition with no penalty.	
Rooming List / Reservation Due Date	[insert actual date]
Will be fourteen (14) days prior to contracted arrival date	

Room Cancellation

Should our Organization cancel this Agreement and if our Organization pays any cancellation fee, liquidated damages or penalty to Hotel, the amount paid will be credited 100% against any charges incurred by our Organization and / or such party as designated by our Organization, and owed to Hotel for any meeting, event or banquet booked within twelve (12) months after the Start Date of the originally scheduled meeting.

Room Cancellation			
Program Dates	Insert actual dates	Cancellation % of liquidated sleeping room damages	Amount Due
6+ months prior to Start Date	[Month, day, year]	0%	$0
4-5 months prior to Start Date		25%	$
2-3 months prior to Start Date		50%	$
0-1 month prior to Start Date		75%	$

Here is another copy of a form that Debi created to be used with Hotel Contracts:

(Client) Attrition and Cancellation for (Name of Meeting)

Attrition Calculation			
Total number of rooms	1,565		
% Attrition	20%		
Rooms allowed to decrease	313		
Room Block with Attrition	1,252		
Food and Beverage	$300,000		
Food and Beverage attrition reduction			
Rooms Cancellation			
# Rooms with Attrition		1,252	
x Room rate (enter rate)		$225	
Cancellation Amount		$281,700	
Food and Beverage Cancellation			
Total Minimum Revenue		$300,000	
Cancellation by Dates			
Cancellation amount Rooms	100%	$281,700*	July 3 to August 2, 2014 (0-30 days)
F&B	75%	$225,000**	
	Total Owed	$506,700	

Cancellation amount Rooms	75%	$211,275*	
F&B	50%	$150,000	*ADD DATES IN*
	Total Owed	$361,275	(31 – 90 days)
Cancellation amount Rooms	50%	$140,850*	
F&B	0%		*ADD DATES IN*
	Total Owed	$140,850	(91 – 180 days)
Cancellation amount Rooms	25%	$ 70,425*	
F&B	0%		*ADD DATES IN*
	Total Owed	$ 70,425	(181 – 365 days)
Cancellation amount Rooms	5%	$ 14,085*	
F&B	0%		*ADD DATES IN*
	Total Owed	**$ 14,085**	(signing through 366 days)
* deduct rooms resold			
** deduct F&B resold			

Appendix E - Food and Beverage Attrition and Cancellation Grids

Food & Beverage Estimated Costs

Hotel shall provide an estimated, itemized list of food and beverage costs by providing the cost estimates in the table below. This pricing shall be determined based on current menus in effect at contract signing date.

Our Organization recognizes that actual food and beverage costs will be provided by the Hotel after our Organization submits the Meeting specifications. The following table is to be used for estimating costs only.

Our Organization requires that daily function / banquet event orders be reviewed and approved one week prior to the meeting. Each day, the Hotel will provide our Organization with banquet checks for approval and signature prior to posting them to the master account. Banquet checks should include the guarantee as well as the actual number served.

Function	Quantity	# of attendees	Cost per person	Total cost
This table is not necessary if the Hotel provides estimated food and beverage costs through a computer-generated printout.				
Rooms should be located away from elevators, stairwells and ice / soda machines if possible.				
Check-in time expected:				
Check-out time expected:				
Continental Breakfast	insert # of meals	insert # of people	insert actual or average cost	insert total estimated cost
Full Breakfast				
AM Break				
Buffet Lunch				
Plated Lunch				
PM Break				
Reception				
Buffet Dinner				
Plated Dinner				
TOTAL Estimated Food & Beverage				insert total estimated cost
Taxes (if applicable)	%			
Service Charges (if applicable)	%			
Is Service Charge Taxable?	Yes or No			

Debi has created an addendum with key terms and concessions that you will want to include in your hotel contract. Although we have included these sample room, food and beverage attrition and cancellation grids, the contract information can be found online at Debi's blog. We added the attrition and cancellation grids because this information is so important to calculate for your hotel contracts. Ask a hotel to clearly define how much you will owe on the exact date should your attendance fall short of the commitment or if you cancel your meeting. Remember, these terms are negotiable. For more information on hotel contracts, visit www.TEPlus.net.

(Sample) Food & Beverage Cancellation

The following calculations shall apply for Food and Beverage charges if the Event is cancelled:

Food & Beverage Cancellation			
Program Dates	**Insert actual dates**	**Cancellation % of liquidated Food / Beverage damages**	**Amount Due**
Less than 30 days to Start Date	[Month, day, year]	40% of Contracted Estimated Food / Beverage Costs	$
30+ days prior to Start Date	[Month, day, year]	No penalty	NA

The following calculations shall apply for Food and Beverage charges due to attrition:

(Sample) Food & Beverage Attrition

(This language is negotiable with the Hotel). Hotel agrees to allow Organization to reduce the total anticipated food and beverage cumulative amount by 20% without penalty 72 hours prior to the Meeting Date. Minimum food / beverage is a total, cumulative spend for the meeting / event; not a spend per function. Any penalties for reduction beyond the allowable food and beverage attrition will be based on food and beverage profit, not to exceed 40%. If our Organization's food and beverage total is reduced by any amount and is resold by the Hotel to another group, our Organization will only be responsible for the difference between the revenue generated by the Meeting and the food and beverage minimum multiplied by the profit.

Food and Beverage Minimum	
Food and Beverage Minimum:	$
20% allowable attrition	$
Food and Beverage Requirement:	$

How to save money on food and beverages

Professional meeting planners can plan your menus and provide numerous negotiation tips for cost-effective food and beverage options. Some ideas include:

- "I need your help (to stay on budget, to get costs down…)."
- "Can you (and/or your Chef) please work with me on (budget, price, menu goals…)."
- "In the past your company has extended us the courtesy of a 25% discount."
- Compare a la carte pricing vs. package costs; as stated above, use consumption pricing when possible. Instruct the hotels that limited quantities should be placed out at a time, with ample restock readily available and hotel staff to oversee the restocking need.
- Use water coolers or pitchers of water rather than individual water bottles.
- Always negotiate a discount on food and beverage; 20% is common.
- Unless your event is primarily catering, your food & beverage budget should not exceed 30% of the total meeting budget / spend, excluding airfare, content development, and delivery. If your meeting requires attendees to share rooms (double-occupancy), then your hotel costs will be less and food and beverage allotment should not exceed 38-40% of the total meeting budget / spend.
- Negotiate with your hotel property to ensure that food and beverage minimums are in line with your total expenses, but do not agree to increasing room rentals or other charges to replace food and beverage revenue. When calculating your food and beverage minimums, only take meals into consideration, not breaks. Calculate the minimums using the lowest priced meal option.
- You may want to under-guarantee your food and beverage amount even more than the calculations above. Some organizations under-guarantee the attendance by 50% for breakfast; 15% for lunch and 20% for dinner, unless there is networking with dinner, then under-guarantee the dinner by 15%.
- Some organizations have opted to eliminate continental breakfast altogether and allow a $20 limit for attendees to order room service. Obviously, the $ limit would be based on the norm for the city.
- Provide boxed lunch on the closing day of the meeting / event and / or for opening day at meetings that begin at noon.
- Eliminate desserts at lunch. If dessert price is included at lunch, serve it for the afternoon break.
- Eliminate breakfast served for programs that begin at 9:00 a.m. or later.
- Forego receptions when they occur before a meal function.
- Provide 1 or 2 nights as "on own" with $30-40 pre-paid dinners at hotel outlets during multi-day learning programs.
- Separate dessert costs from dinner – only order half of the amount of desserts.

- Limit open bars to 2 hours.
- Distribute drink tickets (2 per person) at all meetings that include staff with less than a manager title.
- Serve beer and wine only for all meetings that include staff with less than a manager title.
- Limit hospitality suites to 2 hours.
- Use water stations with servers pouring out of large water bottles.
- Contact chefs directly. Challenge them to be creative within your budget and to work with your meeting's goals and concept.
- Do not use set menus, except as a guideline.
- Buy coffee and tea in bulk or by the gallon, if possible.
- Serve whole fruit, not sliced.
- Cut down on portions. Cut Danishes and doughnuts in half. Offer mini-muffins, mini-doughnuts, and mini-Danishes. Not everyone wants to eat the whole pastry. Offer them the option to indulge without the guilt of leaving half on their plate.

Appendix F – Sample Alcohol Guidelines

Guidelines for Serving Alcohol at Organization-Sponsored Meetings and / or Events

<u>For the Event Planner or Meeting Sponsor</u>

Individuals who are under the influence of alcohol at an Organization's meeting or event may engage in behavior that is inconsistent with our values, presents a poor or unfavorable image of themselves and / or the Organization or, in some circumstances, can cause risk to themselves and / or the Organization.

As an event planner or meeting sponsor, you may have decided, or been directed, to include alcoholic beverages at an upcoming event or meeting.

This document is intended to provide you with considerations and guidance regarding the serving and use of alcohol at Organization meetings or events.

Serving Alcoholic Beverages

- Hire a third-party vendor (hotel, caterer, etc.) to serve alcoholic beverages on our Organization's premises or at Organization-sponsored events or meetings, including private parties at residences if the Organization is sponsoring and / or funding the event. The Organization should not do anything but host a function: it should not sell or serve any of the alcoholic beverages that are consumed at an Organization meeting or event.

- "Self-service" alcohol <u>is not permitted</u>. Whether in hospitality suites or other settings, the lack of control or ability to monitor consumption increases the level of risk associated with the event.

- Limit attendance to Organization's employees and invited guests. The event or meeting may not be open to the public.

- Consider the participant makeup (i.e., staff level) and event / meeting type in determining the types of alcoholic beverages (e.g., beer, wine, liquor) to be served by the third-party vendor.

- Consider serving only beer / wine for events consisting mainly of Associates, Sr. Associates.

As a matter of guidance, an Organization-sponsored meeting / event with an open bar should not extend longer than three hours. As a general rule, no extensions to serving hours will be made once on-site. However, upon notice to the facility / hotel person responsible for the Organization's event / meeting, an identified Organization individual (the Organization's meeting sponsor or another responsible individual) can be authorized to extend the serving hours if he / she deems it appropriate to do so.

At events where individuals are responsible for driving to their homes or hotels, have available alternate means of transportation for anyone who appears unable to drive or is identified as such by the third-party vendor.

In-Office Events

Small celebratory events (e.g., anniversaries, birthdays, passing an Organization-sponsored exam, retirements) where limited amounts of alcohol may be served frequently occur in Organization offices. At such events, the quantity of alcohol available should allow for no more than 1-2 drinks per person as a token in honor of the occasion. If the event is larger, a third-party vendor as mentioned above should be hired. <u>These are the only types of events where alcohol is permitted without a third-party vendor serving.</u>

Consumption of alcohol may not be permitted per your Organization office lease. Please consult with your Office Service Manager before any events are planned.

Events at Organization's Staff Homes

Staff must be aware that their personal liability insurance will be primary for events sponsored at their homes in the event of a loss. All alcoholic beverage guidelines must be considered when arranging an event at a Staff's home.

Off-site Happy Hours

Limit office-arranged happy hours to a two-hour maximum. Never leave an "open tab" available for those who might want to continue a happy hours event after the time allotted for it has ended.

Communication with Attendees. If there is a written communication for the event that includes information regarding logistics (e.g., transportation, dress code), or pre-event materials with that type of information, consider including a section entitled "Alcohol Use Guidance" that may read:

Drink Responsibly

Alcoholic beverages are often provided at Organization meetings and events. As an employee of our Organization, you have a responsibility to conduct yourself in a professional and appropriate manner – particularly when alcohol is being consumed. Whether it's during the meeting or after the event at a local bar, your behavior is a direct reflection on the Organization. Enjoy yourself, but don't let too much drink sink your career.

At events where there are large numbers of junior-level staff, event sponsors might consider remarks at the opening of the event stressing the importance of maintaining professional conduct throughout the entire event, even when the "official" activities have concluded for a particular day.

Other Considerations / Guidance

The Organization's "Host Liquor Liability" insurance covers the Organization for any functions where alcoholic beverages are offered as long as the Organization is not selling or serving the beverages.

Ensure that facilities, establishments or other venues where an Organization meeting or event will take place have "Liquor Liability" insurance for when they sell / serve the liquor at bars, restaurants and functions. Bartenders and servers should be trained in serving alcohol. As a planner, you should ensure that indeed they are.

Obtain and maintain a copy – preferably electronic – of the Certificate of Insurance from the third-party vendor.

Ensure that the contract between Organization and the facility, establishment or other venue where our Organization's meeting or event will take place provides that:

a. It has a current license to dispense alcoholic beverages.

b. The owner assumes control of alcohol sales and service.

c. Bartenders and servers are trained and instructed in accordance with local laws and regulations to identify and refuse service to intoxicated attendees.

d. It agrees to carry a minimum of two million dollars in liquor liability insurance and further agrees that all of its employees and agents performing services under the contract shall at all times comply with all federal, state, and local laws pertaining to the sale, service or furnishing of alcoholic beverages.

e. Its employees and agents shall not sell or serve alcoholic beverages to anyone attending the meeting / function who is under twenty-one years of age or to anyone, regardless of age, who is visibly intoxicated.

f. It agrees to indemnify and hold our Organization harmless with respect to any and all claims, losses, damages, liabilities, judgments, or settlements, including reasonable attorney's fees, costs, and other expenses incurred by Organization on account of any liquor related activities conducted by the facility / establishment pursuant to the contract.

Do not allow the Hotel / Facility to add additional "limitation of liability" language to any contract. If you have any questions on the supplier contract, contact the Meeting Planner or the Office of General Counsel immediately.

If you become aware of in-office celebrations where alcohol is served, consider passing the guidance above to the event planner or meeting sponsor.

Please be aware of the fact that this guidance will be sent to all the local office leaders to ensure that in-office events where alcohol is served are conducted in accordance herewith. Feel free to remind local offices when necessary if you become aware of any such celebration.

These guidelines pertain to all Organization events and meetings including Recruiting, Marketing meetings / events, and outings.

Appendix G – Room Setups

Room Setup

Room setup is determined based upon the format and objective of the meeting. When you identify your room and the proper setup, consider the following:

- Put the podium or head table opposite the entry to the room so that incoming participants do not distract the already-seated attendees.
- Locate the temperature and lighting controls to ensure that they are easily accessible.
- Determine if a registration or materials table is needed for the back of the room.
- Determine if a water cooler is needed for the back of the room.
- Determine where easels (if needed) may be placed that may hold pre-printed signage.

Use the following calculators at the following website to determine how many people will fit in your meeting or banquet room or what size room you will need for your number of people attending.

http://www.hotelplanner.com/Common/Popups/SpaceCalculator.cfm

Theater or Auditorium: Attendees sit in row of chairs facing the head table or speaker; best suited for lecture-type meeting. This setup is not recommended when food and beverages are being served in the room or when attendees need to take notes. Rows can be angled, straight, or semi-circular. Another recommendation is to offset each row so that attendees do not have to look directly at the person in front of them, however, additional space may be required for offset rows.

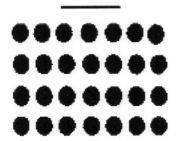 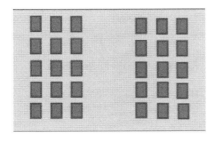 

Schoolroom or Classroom: Attendees sit in row of rectangular tables facing the speaker; also suited for lecture-type meetings, allows for note-taking and attendees with laptops or tablets. A few different classroom setups are possible but the most convenient and spacious setup is with 2 attendees per 6 foot table. This setup is also conducive for food and beverages when needed in the same room.

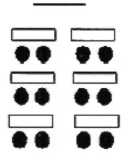 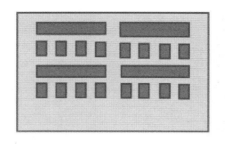 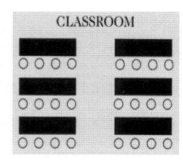

Boardroom / Conference: A rectangular or oval table setup with surrounding chairs used for board meetings, committee meetings, and other small functions at which interaction between participants is expected. Appropriate for interactive discussions and note-taking sessions for fewer than 25 people. If a presentation will be shown on a screen, it is a good idea to leave one end open (using the U-Shape) so that all participants can see the screen. This design also can be used for high-level food and beverage functions with a small number of attendees. The round table is called an Ambassador Table, whereas the rectangular table is called the Royal Table.

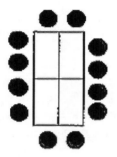 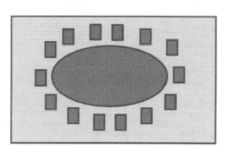 

Hollow Square: A rectangular setup, with rectangular tables arranged in a square design leaving the center empty or "hollow" with surrounding chairs. This setup is good for larger committee or board meetings of 17-30 people, at which interaction among attendees is important. . If a presentation will be shown on a screen, it is a good idea to leave one end open (using the U-Shape) so that all participants can see the screen. This design also can be used for high-level food and beverage functions with a small number of attendees.

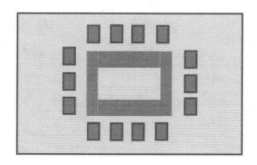 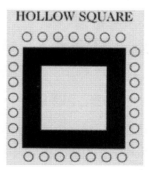

U-shape: This shape is frequently used for Board of Directors meetings, committees or discussions when a presentation is being shown at the open end of the seating. It is appropriate for groups of fewer than 30 people. This design also can be used for high-level food and beverage functions with a small number of attendees.

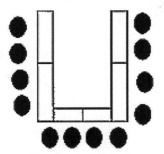 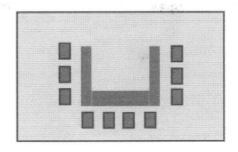 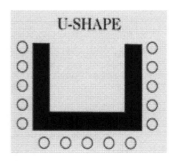

Banquet Style: Frequently used for food and beverage dining activities with 6-10 people sitting at a table. Note that this design does not work well when a speaker is in front of the room because half of the table will not be able to see the speaker.

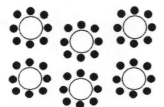 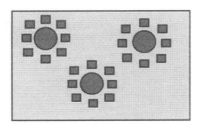 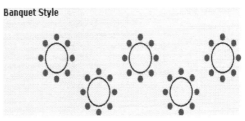

Crescent Rounds: A variation of the full round setup. The two or three chairs in which delegates would have their backs to the speaker are removed, thus forming a "crescent" of seating facing the speaker. This design works well when you need to use a room for meals and an educational session that immediately follows. Recommended to allow attendees to face the stage and participate in table discussions, case studies or small focus groups.

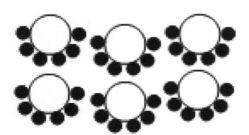 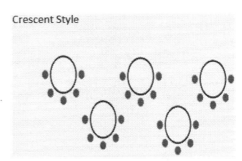

Cocktail or Reception: These small, round cocktail or reception tables can be used with or without chairs. If tall tables are used, they can be stand-up tables; or low tables can include 3-4 chairs.

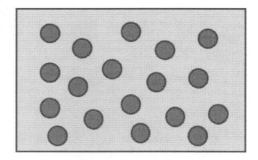

Other table arrangements: There are numerous other table arrangements. Some of them are shown below.

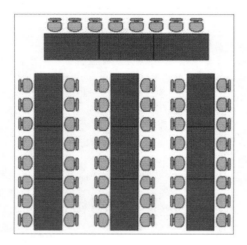

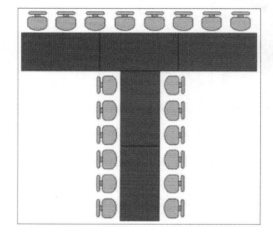

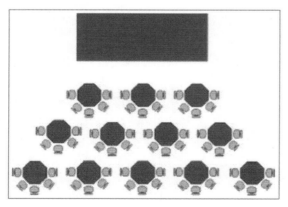

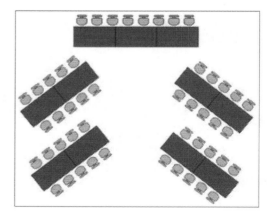

Appendix H – Sample Checklist

The following checklist is NOT in chronological order, but rather grouped by topic. Some tasks may need to be done months in advance and some can be done closer to the meeting.

The best thing to do is to put this document into Excel (contact Debi or Susan if you want an Excel version), add in the dates, and then sort it in Excel by date so that you have a chronological project plan.

MEETING NAME	
DATES	
LOCATION	
PERSON RESPONSIBLE	
ADDITIONAL RESOURCES and their ROLES	

Additional columns that should be added to your Checklist include Date Completed and Person Responsible.

Activity	Target Due Date	Comments
Consulting with the Meeting Sponsor		
Meets with business leader, meeting sponsor or budget holder to get the key questions answered and understand the needs.		
Agree on weekly, bi-weekly, or regular audio conferences or meetings with all stakeholders. Use same dial-in, time, day if possible. Review this checklist during each team meeting and provide updates.		
Sourcing / Contracting		
Provide information to the meeting requester on "avoidance dates" re: key religious holidays, organization closed, etc. if one of those dates are chosen and it isn't obvious by reviewing the calendar.		
Get all of the data needed to begin finding the right location and property.		
Estimate / Benchmark Costs including air.		
Request approval if necessary with estimated meeting costs.		
Receive approval.		
Determine who will do each part of the sourcing and planning / assign staff.		

Activity	Target Due Date	Comments
Let the meeting sponsor know who the key contacts are.		
Request key measurable success factors (to measure business impact of meeting / event).		
Identify decision-maker / final authority and decision making.		
Request budget or help create one.		
Identify and document threats, risks (dates, attendance, instructors, changes, policies, travel, resources, etc.). Escalate if required.		
Update this checklist with all due dates as needed.		
Request air analysis from Group Travel / preferred travel management company (allow 48-72 hours).		
Send out venue RFP (allow 48-72 hours at minimum for a response from the properties). If you have access to a meeting management technology, this can be automated very easily.		
Review and evaluate responses.		
Use responses / prepare cost site analysis.		
Contact Security if applicable to review locations.		
Present options / cost analysis to meeting sponsor.		
Receive customer feedback / approval / or revisions.		
Update cost analysis as recommended.		
Conduct site inspection.		
Ask and document minority business suppliers if factor in decision.		
Make decision on location.		
Negotiate venue contract with IT / Procurement assistance especially if your meeting requester has special IT needs or if the amount is over $25,000.		
Obtain customer approval on contract – may want to use a customer sign-off sheet.		
Document the Venue Contract Due Date.		
Submit negotiated contract to next reviewer and allow the next reviewer a couple of days at least before signing off on the contract.		
Ensure that the right person signs the contract who is on the contract signature matrix (not everyone in an organization is allowed to sign contracts).		
Return signed contract to venue.		
Receive countersigned contract / add to document retention repository.		
Keep a file with everything; preferably, use a meeting management technology to record all of the information. Update meeting profile (attachments, status, financials).		

Activity	Target Due Date	Comments
Submit deposit request (s) (it is recommended that deposits only be paid to non-preferred hotel properties).		
Document Minority Business Suppliers and provide this spend to Procurement as applicable.		
Update meeting sponsor on budget (regularly).		
Update this checklist with all due dates.		
Planning		
Work with meeting sponsor / contact on budget updates.		
Create, share and post all meeting planner, sponsor and stakeholder contact information with names, addresses, phone, cell phone, fax numbers and any other relevant information.		
Update this checklist with all due dates from meeting planners and stakeholders; attach to profile (if using meeting management technology), and share with entire meeting project team.		
Request pricing from preferred ground transportation suppliers for decision-making.		
Contact customer and discuss the logistics planning:		
Reiterate key measurable success factors.		
General sessions / breakouts / other.		
Content Consultation (agenda, objectives).		
Attendee Management.		
Security – consult and obtain information.		
Information Technology / Connectivity / Mobile Apps, etc.		
Speakers / Entertainment.		
Off-site (Destination Management Company needed?).		
Activities / Guest Program.		
Branding / Meeting theme.		
Production / Audio-visual.		
Collateral / printed materials.		
Shipping Requirements (on-site / supplies).		
Ground Transportation.		
Food and Beverage.		
On-site Office Requirements (staff / equipment).		
Communications (with attendees, speakers, sponsors, etc.)		
Continuing Education Credits.		
Incentives / gifts / amenities.		

Activity	Target Due Date	Comments
Get agreement from all stakeholders on timeframe for deliverables by you or other suppliers.		
Agree on cut-off date for technology / attendee registration to be sent and then closed for input.		
Determine if other Meetings Team or other staff members are required for assistance during planning and / or on-site. Identify support – use right skills / job.		
Content Consultation		
Discuss meeting objectives with customer; determine method to capture return on investment.		
Develop meeting flow chart / outline.		
Determine flow of meeting, general session, breakouts.		
Branding / Meeting Theme		
Determine requirements.		
Contact Creative Services.		
Review branding policies.		
Determine what branding requirements will be required for website.		
General Session / Breakouts		
Determine # of participants, timing, flow, requirements, proximity to other sessions, special requirements, minimum and maximum audience sizes, etc.		
Ask if prayer / meditation room / lactation rooms are required.		
Document above requirements, date it, share it, and update with meeting sponsor regularly.		
Determine what requirements / verbiage will be required for technology website development.		
Ensure that technology developer is given ample time to develop.		
Speakers / Entertainment		
Gather options.		
Review options or ask customer to review.		
Send request for proposal or select suppliers.		
Review bids if request for proposal was used.		
Ask and document minority business suppliers if a factor in decision.		
Provide summary of all suppliers to customer.		
Select speaker / entertainment.		
Negotiate contract.		
Send negotiated contract to reviewer.		

Activity	Target Due Date	Comments
Document Contract Due Date.		
Obtain countersigned contract and attach to profile in technology system or maintain.		
Determine what requirements / verbiage will be required for website development.		
Confirm requirements / details (air, hotel, A / V, ground, etc.).		
Submit request for deposit.		
Ensure invoice receipt within 30 days or contact.		
Reconcile invoice.		
Submit Payment Request.		
Activities / Guest Programs		
Gather options.		
Review options or ask customer to review.		
Send request for proposal or select activities.		
Review bids if request for proposal was used.		
Ask and document minority business suppliers, if a factor in decision.		
Provide summary to customer.		
Select venue and / or activities.		
Negotiate contract.		
Send negotiated contract to reviewer.		
Document the Contract Due Date.		
Obtain countersigned contract and attach to profile in technology system or maintain.		
Determine what requirements / verbiage will be required for website development.		
Submit request for deposit.		
Ensure invoice receipt within 30 days or contact.		
Reconcile invoice.		
Submit Payment Request.		
Off-site Event(s)		
Gather options.		
Participate in event, tasting, etc. to evaluate.		
Send request for proposal or select suppliers.		
Review bids if request for proposal was used.		
Ask and document minority business suppliers, if a factor in decision.		
Provide summary to customer.		

Activity	Target Due Date	Comments
Select venue.		
Negotiate contract.		
Send negotiated contract to next reviewer.		
Document Contract Due Date here.		
Obtain countersigned contract and attach to profile.		
Determine what requirements / verbiage will be required for website development.		
Submit request for deposit.		
Participate in event, tasting, etc. to customize.		
Finalize all off-site details, guarantees, menus, transportation, etc. **NOTE:** Ask Customer how much input they want. Do they want to help select menus? Approve menus? Or leave everything to you?		
Ensure invoice receipt within 30 days or contact.		
Reconcile invoice.		
Submit Payment Request.		
DESTINATION MANAGEMENT COMPANY (DMC) (Follow steps above for activities / guest programs)		
If off-site events / activities above are extensive and require use of DMC, negotiated contracts to be sent to the next reviewer for signature 30 business days in advance of due date.		
Document Contract Due Date here.		
Submit deposit request.		
Ensure invoice receipt within 30 days or contact.		
Reconcile invoice.		
Submit payment request.		
Travel		
Contact the preferred Travel Management Company (TMC) to begin discussing how the attendees will make their air travel reservations, (online booking tool, agent-assisted method), how you will collect arrival and departure manifests so that the ground transportation company can pick up and drop off attendees at the right time.		
Determine if Group Travel or Transient Online Booking tool will be used.		
Determine who will run manifests, how often, in what format. (Will it be the TMC Group Travel Desk?) Is there a cost?		
Document the date(s) that the manifests are expected (every few days? Once a week? Day before the meeting?).		
Determine who will answer policy questions about travel exceptions.		

Activity	Target Due Date	Comments
Determine what requirements / verbiage will be required for website development.		
Receive total airline cost for meeting / program (60 days after program end).		
Security		
Verify locations with Organization's Security Team.		
Obtain venue disaster / emergency contingency plan from hotels / suppliers.		
Use Debi Scholar's Crisis Management Handbook (available on Amazon).		
Determine if additional Security Staff are needed.		
Role play with all onsite staff to be sure they are ready for each Crisis.		
Website Development		
Contact website developer, set up call with sponsor and sourcer / planner to discuss registration options available (When must registration go out to attendees?) Give developer X business days to create website (prefer 5-10).		
Conduct call, discuss options, make decision on best method of registration delivery.		
Send email notification to website developer if registration communication is using the tool, indicate anticipated launch dates.		
Document the anticipated Launch Date here.		
Document the anticipated Registration Close Date here.		
Create meeting / event website in technology tool.		
Create Custom Pages.		
Set Registration Policies.		
Create Contact Fields on registration form.		
Create Registration Form.		
Set Accommodation Policies.		
Create Accommodations Form.		
Set Travel Polices.		
Create travel form or link to online booking tool.		
Review & Update Advanced Option Selections.		
Activate Website.		
Test Website (Administrator Testing).		
Distribute for Team Testing.		
Receive Feedback from Testing.		
Update Website from Feedback.		

Activity	Target Due Date	Comments
Distribute Website for Registration.		
Grant Access to Website (outside of meetings team).		
Review data and ensure registration is functioning correctly.		
Train meeting sponsor or other staff on how to pull & create custom reports.		
Create scheduled Reports (if needed).		
Review weekly or daily registration reports.		
Archive Website in technology tool.		
Information Technology		
Meet with IT to determine requirements and resourcing.		
Provide cost estimates to customer.		
A / V / Production		
Identify A / V / Production requirements.		
Identify virtual meeting requirements.		
Send AV specifications questionnaire to instructors / presenters.		
Determine if audience response system or other technologies is required.		
Research vendors including the national vendors (if applicable).		
Create / determine diagrams for request for proposal.		
Send out request for proposal.		
Review bids if request for proposal was used.		
Ask and document minority business suppliers, if a factor in decision.		
Select vendor.		
Negotiate contract.		
Send negotiated contracts to next reviewer.		
Contract Due Date.		
Obtain countersigned contract and attach to meeting file in the meeting management technology or maintain it.		
Submit deposit request.		
Work with customer and production co. to develop presentation template and staging.		
Consult with Marketing as needed.		
Coordinate any pre-meeting video shoots.		
Obtain certificate of insurance, security access, etc.		
Coordinate presentations and staging (receive presentations, review for consistency and redundancy, give to production co.).		
Review final presentations for errors, consistency, spelling, etc.		

Activity	Target Due Date	Comments
Update diagrams / requirements as needed.		
Develop and coordinate graphics materials.		
Ensure that the organization's branded colors work well with AV and production – true colors.		
Develop and coordinate rehearsal schedule.		
Develop and coordinate Director's Agenda.		
Coordinate internal requirements, technology booths, etc.		
Coordinate General Session requirements with production company (manage flow of show).		
Document and share schedule for load-in, crew meals, security, etc.		
Document and share production company room requirements, travel schedules, etc.		
Schedule edits or additional video shoots as necessary.		
Ensure invoice receipt within 30 days or contact.		
Reconcile invoice.		
Submit payment request.		
Gifts / Incentives / Amenities		
Determine requirements.		
Determine budget.		
Research vendors / use organization's gift shop.		
Present options to customer.		
Order gifts.		
Submit deposit request.		
Coordinate delivery to site.		
Reconcile vendor invoice if applicable.		
Pay final invoice.		
Collateral / Print Materials		
Determine requirements.		
Contact Creative Services or other.		
Receive all requirements from customer.		
Receive sample from Creative Services or other.		
Provide draft to customer.		
Receive customer approval.		
Coordinate production with Creative Services or other.		
Provide 5-10 bus. days for Creative Services or other for return.		
Coordinate delivery to site.		

Activity	Target Due Date	Comments
Submit deposit request.		
Ensure invoice receipt within 30 days or contact.		
Reconcile vendor invoice if applicable.		
Submit payment request.		
Shipping Requirements (on-site / supplies)		
Inquire if Shipping Services will be needed.		
Determine if Shipping Services is required on-site or just supplies.		
Submit form to Shipping Services with requests.		
Coordinate scheduling with Shipping Services.		
Ground Transportation		
Determine requirements.		
Send out requests for proposal or select supplier.		
Review bids if request for proposal was used.		
Provide summary to customer.		
Select vendor from preferred vendors only unless exception granted.		
Negotiate contract.		
Send negotiated contract to next reviewer.		
Contract Due Date.		
Submit deposit request.		
Provide ground transportation information for registration.		
Provide manifest / final specs.		
Manage changes.		
Oversee on-site / Act as dispatch if needed.		
Ensure invoice receipt within 30 days or contact.		
Reconcile invoice.		
Submit payment request.		
Capture and report transportation issues in the problem / resolution repository.		
Food and Beverage		
Discuss requirements with customer. This info should come back on registration from attendees but be prepared to have Muslim Halal meals, Kosher meals, vegetarian meals, and other diet-restrictive meals on hand.		
Obtain venue menus. **NOTE:** Ask Customer how much input they want. Do they want to help select menus? Approve menus? Or, leave everything to us?		

Activity	Target Due Date	Comments
Identify how to make meals "healthy" so that you're offering a variety of options.		
Consult with venue chef (if applicable).		
Negotiate menu pricing.		
Provide venue with requirements.		
Provide venue with special meal requests.		
Submit guarantees.		
Receive Banquet Event Orders (BEOs).		
Review BEO's (also in meeting specs).		
Share final BEO's with customer.		
Sign and return BEO's.		
Ask the venue to use labels to differentiate food (allergies, etc.) if buffet.		
Determine and communicate special dietary needs.		
Attach BEO's to meeting profile if using a meeting management technology.		
Rooming List		
Prepare draft rooming list from technology tool or other reports.		
Ensure billing information is correct for all attendees.		
Prepare rooming list (singles / doubles, etc.).		
Submit rooming list.		
Confirm VIPs.		
Guarantee / release rooms as required.		
Update rooming list daily / weekly or as needed.		
On-site Requirements		
Determine equipment and staff requirements.		
Contact IT / Security / Other with requirements.		
Order equipment.		
Order and ship supplies.		
Contact Shipping Services and order shipping supplies.		
Recruit office staff.		
Assign roles and responsibilities.		
Determine staff schedules.		
Decide and order staff shirts / uniforms.		
Communicate schedules.		
Meeting Specs		
Finalize agenda.		

Activity	Target Due Date	Comments
Confirm A / V requirements.		
Prepare meeting specs.		
Prepare breakout assignments.		
Receive approval on meeting specs.		
Submit meeting specs.		
Finalize details (list if required).		
Communications		
Between planner and sponsor:		
Project plan.		
Budget from sponsor.		
Billing instructions.		
Final costs to sponsor.		
Invitation list.		
Final agenda.		
CE Requirements / documentation.		
Meeting specifications.		
Regularly scheduled project team calls with minutes.		
Registration website information.		
Manage registration (cut off, deadlines, inquiries).		
Manifests.		
Rooming list.		
Debrief.		
Between sponsor and participants:		
Hold the date.		
Launch registration.		
Communications / memos		
Registration reminders.		
Confirmations.		
Evaluations.		
Between planner and venue:		
Pre-con with hotel staff.		
Tip cards.		
Post-con with hotel staff.		
Billing instructions.		
Confirm that enough space is provided for meals.		
Set up office.		

Activity	Target Due Date	Comments
Test printers, copiers and high speed connectivity.		
Set up shipping area for participants.		
Confirm general session / breakout requirements for A / V.		
Assist with rehearsal for A / V.		
Pack supplies / ship.		
Meet with hotel contacts for meeting updates.		
Ask hotel staff assistance in getting participants into sessions after breaks and meals.		
Review charges / bill and sign off.		
On-site Checklist		
Ensure that specs and BEOs are accurate.		
Review rooming list.		
Check on VIP rooms.		
Coordinate with Guest Services delivery of amenities or other gifts.		
Request keys for all rooms that must be secured.		
Conduct pre-con meeting and tour with hotel and other staff.		
Conduct pre-con meeting with the on-site meetings team.		
Ensure that walkie-talkies are available and operational.		
Document numbers for Catering, Sales, A / V, other important #s.		
Review classroom setup for room numbers, space, A / V, special requests.		
Confirm that shredders are in place.		
Confirm that F&B meet specs, quality, temperature, variety and that labels are used for allergies, etc.		
Confirm that special meals / dietary requirements are met.		
Confirm that enough space is provided for meals.		
Set up office.		
Test printers, copiers and high-speed connectivity.		
Set up shipping area for participants.		
Confirm general session / breakout requirements for A / V.		
Confirm that A / V / Production presentations are error-free if required.		
Run rehearsals with speaker / production co. if required.		
Communicate changes with A / V / Production as required.		
Pack supplies / ship.		
Meet with hotel contacts for meeting updates.		
Ask hotel staff assistance in getting participants into sessions after breaks and meals.		

Activity	Target Due Date	Comments
Review charges / bill and sign off.		
Post-meeting		
Conduct post-con.		
Debrief with customer.		
Post debrief form in Meetings File.		
Take advantage of coaching opportunities – giving or receiving. Ask for coaching.		
Send Meetings Team survey to meeting sponsor.		
Ask Meeting Sponsor for copy of completed participant survey synopsis or analysis (specifically on meetings components).		
Financial		
Submit additional deposit request(s).		
Enter cost avoidance in profile.		
Accrue OR, Pay 90% OR, Pay 100%.		
Prepare, send and post after-meeting analysis report including actual costs compared to budgeted costs.		
UPDATE Program Profile with all relevant information.		
Reconcile all invoices.		
Reporting		
Extract all metrics from the reporting systems, which may include the meeting management technology, the travel management company reports, the T&E system, the compliance system, etc.		
Create reports.		
Calculate the return on investment.		
Analyze reports.		
Create report synopsis and identify opportunities for improvement.		
Distribute reports.		
END		

Appendix I – 75+ Questions to Plan a Meeting

1. What is the meeting objective?
2. What is the general purpose of the meeting?
3. What do you hope to accomplish?
4. What is the expected outcome and how will it be measured?
5. Do you require a baseline of information before the meeting / event starts so that you can compare the information to the after-meeting / event results?
6. What type of meeting is it?
7. Who are the Attendees?
8. Is the meeting / event "open" or "invitation only?"
9. How many attendees are expected?
10. How many attendees will require room nights?
11. Will attendees make their own reservation directly with the hotel or will you collect the RSVPs and provide a rooming list to the hotel?
12. When do you want to hold the meeting? (check national and interfaith holidays)
13. Do you have a second choice of dates?
14. How many days is your meeting?
15. What are the preferred days, month, and year the meeting will be held?
16. What is the lead-time before the meeting?
17. Where do you want to hold the meeting? Information requested: (region, city, state, central location)
18. Where are the attendees coming from?
19. Are all attendees local (able to drive in?)
20. Are attendees regional (limited need for air travel?)
21. Are attendees situated across the country or the world (most requiring air travel?)
22. Are there hotels or venues to which you would like to send a request for proposal?
23. Is it possible to consider using a facility that offers a Complete Meeting Package (CMP) rate which is all-inclusive and usually, less costly than a hotel?
24. Are there penalty credits available for use?
25. What is the budget?
26. Will you be paying for everything? Or only partial expenses if attendees are contributing?
27. Do you have historic data from previous, similar meetings that you can use?

28. Do you have a meeting management technology system that you can use to create and store the budget? Do we need a mobile app? Do we need RFID? Do we need more bandwidth?

29. Have you considered the costs of the venue / hotel sleeping rooms and room rental (if applicable), content, transportation (air, ground), audio-visual equipment, technology, food and beverages, shipping, print materials, security, on-site support, tax / gratuities?

30. What form of payment will be used? Will we have to pay deposits? Will we have to fill out a direct bill application?

31. Will the room and tax be billed to a master account or will each attendee be required to pay for their own expenses?

32. Will the attendees be required to submit a Travel and Entertainment Expense report for the meeting expenses?

33. What is the proposed daily agenda (Registration, General Session, Breakouts, Meals, Breaks, Social Activities, Evening Events, Other?

34. Will the attendees all be arriving on the same day or different days?

35. What type of activities would you like to include? If your activities are held off-site, then this information can be determined after the hotel contract is signed. However, if you require special activities that will affect the cost of the hotel contract, then it is important to discuss these activities before signing the hotel contract.

36. What ethical practices should be followed?

37. How are suppliers selected?

38. Is a site visit to the property or venue needed?

39. Are meeting planner points collected? And, if so, how are they used?

40. Should we consider using suppliers that are registered as a diverse? E.g. minority owned, woman-owned, etc.

41. Should we consider using a supplier who supports our green meeting efforts?

42. Are you prepared to commit to signing a contract to hold the meeting?

43. Who from your organization is allowed to sign a hotel or other type of contract?

44. Has someone from your legal or procurement department reviewed the contract?

45. Are you prepared to commit to an accurate number of attendees?

46. What type of reporting do you need? Consider: volume statistics, attendee and / or budget holder customer satisfaction, budgeted costs vs. actual expenses, cost per person per day. Note that there are numerous types of reports possible.

47. Are there policies or rules that should be followed (e.g., allowable business or first-class travel, single rooms vs. shared rooms, limited number of employees on the same plane)?

48. How are exceptions going to be handled?

49. What type of technology will facilitate the meeting sourcing and planning process?

50. What functionality does the meeting technology offer?

51. Do we need a mobile app?

52. Do we need an audience response system?

53. What types of communications are needed? (attendees, suppliers, speakers, support staff)

54. How many resources are required; for sourcing, pre-planning, on-site, financial reconciliation, website development, etc.)?

55. Where will the resources come from (e.g., internal people, consultants, suppliers, or a hybrid approach of both)?

56. Who will be working with me from the hotel after the contract is signed? (the sales person will turn the file over to a Convention Services Manager).

57. How will I know what meeting rooms I have been assigned or selected?

58. What else should I tell the hotel, or should they be asking me?

59. Are we confident in the room set-up?

60. Will catered meals / breaks be offered? Which meals / breaks?

61. Will we use sit-down, plated service or buffets?

62. Do we need box lunches for the day of departure?

63. Will we have a reception before dinner?

64. Will alcohol be served?

65. Will any meals be taking place off-property (at a place other than the meeting venue)?

66. Is there a minimum amount of money we need to spend on food and beverage?

67. Is there a limit as to how many of our organization's passengers may be on one aircraft?

68. What travel management company or agency do we use? Can we use the meeting planning company's agency?

69. Do we need ground transportation to pick up attendees from the airport? Return attendees to the airport?

70. Should we use the hotel's audio-visual supplier? Or a different audio-visual supplier?

71. Should we load the presentations on to our own laptops? Should we rent laptops?

72. Should we load presentations from one server onto the laptops? Or individually machine by machine?

73. Will attendees pay their own hotel bill and incidentals? Or, will the room and tax be master billed with incidentals going to their corporate card? Or, everything master billed?

74. Do we want to give out gifts, incentives, or amenities? To whom?

75. What will we do if there is a crisis during our meeting?

76. Do we have a Crisis Management Team in our organization? Do we have all of their contact information?

77. Do we want to do a pre-survey and then a post-survey of the topic to be able to identify the improvement? (or ROI?)

78. What could we have done better?

Appendix J - Important Numbers

TRANSPORTATION (numbers verified 9/12)

Flight Stats: http://www.flightstats.com to track flight status and airport delays.

Travel Management Company 24 / 7 Phone Number: _____

Travel Management Company website: _____

Travel Management Company primary contact and phone number for Group Travel: _____

Airlines	Airlines	Car Rental	Greyhound
Air Canada (888) 247-2262	Porter Airlines (888) 619-8622	Ace (317) 248-5686	214-849-8966 7am-7pm CST M-F www.greyhound.com
Alaska Air (800)-252-7522	Southwest (800) 435-9792	Alamo (800) 222-9075	
Allegiant Air (702) 505-8888	Spirit Air (800) 772-7117	Avis (800) 331-1212	
American (800) 433-7300	Sun Country (800) 359-6786	Budget (800)527-0700	
Air Tran (800) 247-8726	United (800) 864-8331	Dollar (800) 800-4000	Amtrak
Delta (800) 221-1212	US Airways (800) 428-4322	Enterprise (800) 261-7331	(800)872-7245
Frontier (800) 432-1359	Virgin America (877) 359-8474	Hertz (800) 654-3131	www.amtrak.com
Jet Blue (800) 538-2583	WestJet (888) 937-8538	National (877) 222-9058	
		Payless (800) 729-5377	
		Thrifty (800) 847-4389	

HOTEL CHAINS

(Preferred Chain #1)	(Preferred Chain #2)	(Preferred Chain #3)
(Global Sales Rep name)	(Global Sales Rep name)	(Global Sales Rep name)
(Phone Number and Email)	(Phone Number and Email)	(Phone Number and Email)

GROUND TRANSPORTATION

(Ground Transportation Co. #1)	(Ground Transportation Co. #2)	(Ground Transportation Co. #3)
(Contact Name)	(Contact Name)	(Contact Name)
(Phone Number and Email)	(Phone Number and Email)	(Phone Number and Email)

PASSPORTS/VISAS

Universal Passport & Visas	International Visa Service	A Briggs Passport & Visa Expeditors
http://www.upvhq.com/	http://ivsdc.com/	http://www.abriggs.com/
(800) 831-2098	(800) 222-8472	(800) 806-0581

OTHER IMPORTANT CONTACTS

USA Embassy Links www.usembassy.gov

Department of Homeland Security www.dhs.gov

World Health Organization www.who.int

U.S. Centers for Disease Control and Prevention www.cdc.gov (800) 232-4636

Flu.Gov www.flu.gov

FEMA (800) 621-3362 Click here for FEMA State Office web Links

Red Cross www.redcross.org 1-800-733-2767

WEATHER	
National Weather Service http://www.weather.gov/	The Weather Channel www.weather.com

NEWS AFFILIATES			
ABC www.abcnews.go.com	CBS www.cbsnews.com	NBC www.nbcnews.com	CNN www.cnn.com

EMERGENCY NUMBERS
Organization's Main Office Number:
Organization's Security Office Number:

Crisis Management Team			
Resource	Cell phone	Main phone	Email
Meeting Planning Leader			
Travel Leader			
Operations / Finance Leader (to oversee processes, secure funds)			
Security Leader			
H.R. Leader / Ethics Liaison			
Legal / Compliance Leader			
Communications Leader			
Information Technology			
Real Estate Leader			
Clergy			
Suppliers: Hotel Ground Offsites			
Others			

Appendix K – Content for your Meeting

Meeting Design/Strategy

The most important part of any meeting or event is ensuring that the attendees leave believing their time at the meeting was useful, productive and worth it. Meetings and Events are held for one or more of these seven reasons:

- Communicate
- Motivate
- Educate
- Celebrate
- Evaluate
- Generate Revenue
- Regenerate the workforce through Recruiting.

Whatever the Organization wants to accomplish, it typically fits into one or more of these categories.

In today's environment, we have four generations of workers: Traditionalist, Baby Boomer, Generation X, and Generation Y, also known as Millennials. Each of these generations has different expectations of success. In addition, we have numerous attendees from different cultures, which affect the a) content and b) delivery media. We are mindful of who attends, their expectations, and how to provide the most valuable experiences based on these factors.

Attendees need to feel engaged and excited about the content regardless of the seven reasons to hold a meeting. Whether it is to communicate or educate, it is important for the whole team (leaders and attendees), to immerse themselves in the meeting or event.

George Bernard Shaw said, "The single biggest problem in communication is the illusion that it has taken place." And, before you identify the activities for the meeting, you must learn about the Organization's culture, people, generations, and strategies.

Consider using an attendee progressive immersion model, when appropriate, to engage attendees and measure the returns.

Meetings and Events
Attendee Engagement

Attendee Progressive Immersion		
Pre-meeting / event	**During meeting / event**	**After meeting / event**
Identify meeting/event tangible objectives to measure ROI; pre-work, marketing / communication campaign including social networking; social interactions with attending colleagues; suppliers	Download presentations; mobile app; chat; web links; file sharing; polling; integrate virtual attendees into face-to-face meeting (aka hybrid); use secure iPads per person to engage attendees with content (all reportable)	On-demand, archived sessions, social networking, share list of attendees, follow up on survey / poll requests or concerns, follow up with attendees to evaluate the use of content to report ROI, reports / analysis
Frequent Involvement		

Make your Meeting / Event Content Ongoing for Improved Results

©Debi Scholar. 2013

If you need to add teambuilding or content for your meeting, sometimes called the Meeting Architecture, then develop a description of what you hope to accomplish.

For example:

- A description of your organization's function, structure, mission and values
- A statement of the aims and functions of the part of the organization's for help (e.g. Business Unit, Department, etc.)
- Where appropriate, a background note to set the proposed project in the context of organizational, training or functional changes (e.g. teambuilding, strategy development, etc.)
- Clearly stated objectives for the projects based on a full definition of the need / problem
- Outcome required
- An outline of the broad approach expected and your required timescale and timetable
- An indication of any other constraints
- Details of any particular skills and experience you think are required for the project
- Details of any other information you require

For the content delivered - ask the supplier to specify:

- Whether the course material already exists or has to be developed
- Development time and costs
- That the consultant will take responsibility for clearing any copyright issues
- How many courses are to run, where, and of what duration
- Dates and elapsed time
- If prerequisite information is needed
- What training equipment is required and who will supply
- Who will supply course documentation and handouts
- What support is required of you and organization (e.g. venue booking)
- The situation regarding copyright of materials developed for your organization
- What familiarization facilities the consultant expects / needs
- How the consultant proposes to learn what they need to know about your organization and the target audience
- How the results of the training are to be evaluated

Following is a list of Debi's favorite suppliers for motivational speakers, four generations in the workplace, teambuilding, and development activities:

- The Mark of Leader: (http://www.themarkofaleader.com/showreel/)
- Team Building Activities: (http://www.bestteambuilding.com/)
- Smart Hunts High Tech Events (http://www.smarthunts.com)
- Afterburner Seminars: (http://www.afterburnerseminars.com/)
- Keppler Speakers Bureau (http://www.kepplerspeakers.com)
  – Note that Debi's favorite speaker is Jaimie Clarke
- Nancy Vogl Speakers Bureau (http://www.NancyVoglSpeakers.com)
- Bridgeworks / Generational Speakers: (http://www.generations.com/)

Appendix L – Resources

Travel and Entertainment Plus Blog (with numerous templates for Meeting Managers (www.TEPlus.net)

Meeting Professionals International (www.mpiweb.org)

Accepted Practices Exchange
(http://www.conventionindustry.org/StandardsPractices/APEX.aspx)

Green Meeting Industry Council (http://www.gmicglobal.org/)

Corporate Meetings and Incentives Magazine (http://meetingsnet.com/corporate-meetings)

Meetings and Conventions Magazine (http://www.meetings-conventions.com/)

Meeting Room Size Calculator
http://www.hotelplanner.com/Common/Popups/SpaceCalculator.cfm

Corbin Ball's Tips and Tools
http://www.corbinball.com

Return on Investment for Meetings / Events (http://www.eventroi.org/roi-week/faculty/)

ASCAP Music License
(http://www.ascap.com/licensing/types/conventions-expos-trade-shows.aspx)

BMI Music License (http://www.bmi.com/licensing/)

Emily Post Business Etiquette
http://www.emilypost.com/business-etiquette

Business Culture on the World Stage
http://www.worldbusinessculture.com/

SmartSource Computer and Audio Visual (www.smartsource.com)

Crowd Compass Mobile Application
(www.crowdcompass.com)

APEX Bandwidth Calculator
http://www.conventionindustry.org/StandardsPractices/APEX/bandwidthconnectivity/bwidthestimator.aspx

Dinova
http://www.dinova.net/

MORE Books, Information, and Tools by Debi and Susan

- **"Crisis Management Handbook: A Quick Reference Guide for Meeting Planners"** by Debi Scholar and Susan Losurdo, 2013, available on Amazon and iTunes
- **"Strategic Meetings Management: Your SMM Toolkit"** by Debi Scholar, 2013, available on Amazon and iTunes
- **"Strategic Meetings Management: The Strategy Quick Reference Guide"** by Debi Scholar, 2010, available on Amazon and iTunes

Available on www.TEPlus.net published by Debi Scholar

2013

- "Strategic Meetings Management: Master Hotel Contracts"
- "Meetings Management Technology: An RFP for Services"
- "62 Opportunities to Save Money on Meetings and Events"
- "Meeting Management Company Pricing Secrets and Toolkit"
- "Powerful Meeting Policy Toolkit"
- "Do it Yourself for Service Level Agreements and Key Performance Indicators" aka "DIY for SLAs and KPIs"

2012

- "Strategic Meetings Management: An RFP for Services"
- "Creating a Virtual Meeting and Event Strategy"
- "Demystifying Return on Investment (ROI) in meetings and events"
- "Hotel Contracts in an SMM Environment: A Contracting Maturity Model"
- "Strategic Meetings Management Business Plan"

2011

- "Measuring the Value of the 7 Types of Meetings"
- "Capture Regulatory Compliance Data in Meetings and Events"
- "Develop a Compliance Strategy"
- "Strategic Meetings Management: The History by Debi Scholar,"

- "Getting a Baseline for your Current State Meetings Analysis"
- "What is the Cost of Change?"
- "Meeting Technology: Is it designed for Meeting Planners or Meeting Directors?"
- "Travel Managers: Don't forget Group Travel"
- "Strategic Meetings Management Presentation"
- "Strategic Meetings Management: Become a Performance and Value Consultant"
- "How Long Does it Take to Plan a Meeting?"
- "The Return on Investment (ROI) in Meetings and Events"
- "Strategic Meetings Management: Putting Yourself in Their Shoes: 35+ Questions for Stakeholders"
- "Virtual Meetings and Events: The 20+ Roles and Responsibilities of the Virtual Meeting Planner" .
- "Strategic Meetings Management: 20 Questions to Choose the Right Resource Model"

2010

- "40 Meeting Complexity Factors"
- "Benchmark Your Strategic Meetings Management Program"
- "Strategic Meetings Management Range Anxiety"
- "Strategic Meetings Management: 80 Components to a Meetings Policy"
- "Travel and Meetings: Use Change Management to Drive Compliance"
- "Strategic Meetings Management: Maturity Model and Strategy Articulation Map"
- "Benefits of Outsourcing Meetings and Events"
- "20 Reasons to Consider Virtual Meetings"
- "How to Negotiate your Corporate Card Terms"
- "Strategic Meetings Management is Poetry to my Ears"
- "T&E Fraud and the Impact on Your Business"
- "15 Questions to Begin a Business Case"

2009

- "Corporate Social Responsibility in Travel and Meetings"
- "T&E Leading and Lagging Controls"
- "Virtual Meetings: Eight Motivating Factors"
- "Examine 13 Areas for Travel and Expense Management Optimization"
- "Where do you find T&E Spend?"

- "Demand Transparency in Pricing Models"
- "Conduct Rate Audits to Reduce Costs"
- "Use an Airline Analysis to Determine a Mix of Preferred Airlines"
- "Request to all Internal Auditors: Please review Meetings and Events"
- "What is Meeting Architecture?"
- "How much is a Relationship Worth? Travel ROI"
- "Corporate Dining may Represent 9% of T&E Spend"
- "Career Ideas for e-Learning Instructional Designers"

How to find Debi and Susan:

Debi's blog, T&E Plus (www.TEPlus.net) has been viewed over 40,000 times as of early 2013 and provides information on archived webinars, tools, and guidance on meetings, travel, card and expense management.

Debi started the popular LinkedIn Group titled, "T&E Plus," which has over 2,500 members as of early 2013.

Debi started the popular LinkedIn Group titled "GBTA Strategic Meetings Management Group," which has over 1,000 members as of early 2013.

Debi created the industry's first free Strategic Meetings Management (SMM) Benchmark tool that allows you to score your current SMM operations at www.SMMBenchmark.com.

Debi can be reached at 1-908-304-4954 or at Debi@DebiScholar.com and her LinkedIn profile is at www.linkedin.com/in/dscholar/.

Susan can be reached at salosurdo@gmail.com and her LinkedIn profile is at www.linkedin.com/in/slosurdo.

Made in the USA
Las Vegas, NV
27 July 2022

52184874R00083